W9-BTD-646

THE ROSWELL INCIDENT

CHARLES BERLITZ AND WILLIAM L. MOORE

MJF BOOKS

NEW YORK

Published by MJF Books
Fine Communications
Two Lincoln Square
60 West 66th Street
New York, NY 10023

Library of Congress Catalog Card Number 96-78815
ISBN 1-56731-132-6

Manufactured in the United States of America on acid-free paper

MJF Books and the MJF colophon are trademarks of Fine Creative Media, Inc.

10   9   8   7   6   5   4   3   2   1

Contents

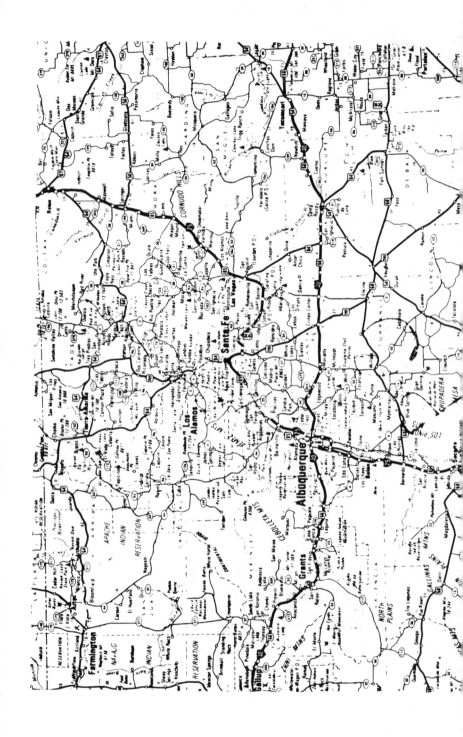

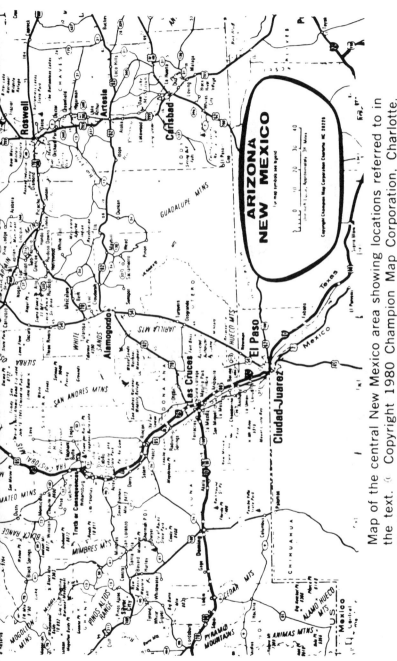

Map of the central New Mexico area showing locations referred to in the text. © Copyright 1980 Champion Map Corporation, Charlotte, North Carolina 28225. All rights reserved.

Introduction

According to UFO legend, an extraterrestrial spaceship crashed in New Mexico in the early days of July 1947. This would seem to be, on the surface, simply another report that has been kept alive in UFO journals and the thousands of books written about UFOs in all languages. What is different about this case, however, is the vitality of this one single incident and its continuing developments in scientific, government, and legal circles.

At the time this book goes to press a civil action has been brought by concerned parties, Citizens Against UFO Secrecy, through their attorneys, against the CIA for the purpose of releasing information about crashed UFOs in accord with the terms of the Freedom of Information Act. CAUS, in addition, has taken over a previous suit of the Ground Saucer Watch against the CIA. Among the charges brought by the suits are suppression of media information, withholding of files, muzzling of witnesses, and, in general, hiding information through the use of now unnecessary security classification.

Events which had been reported in the press and by radio before security regulations were imposed by the Army Air Force (whose name was changed to the Air Force in that very year, 1947) indicate that material from the wrecked UFO was shuttled by high-security government transportation from base to base and that the remains of the UFO *and the dead occupants* (one of whom was reportedly alive when found) are under high-security guard at CIA headquarters at Langley, Virginia.

Those of us who can recall the years before 1947, which was the year of the first well-publicized saucer "invasion," remember reading purportedly factual accounts about what might have been called saucers long before they became popular. These were puzzling reports, carried in meteorological and astronomical journals, containing references to giant airborne objects in the night sky, neither airships nor meteors.

An example from the *Monthly Weather Review* (March 1904):

Lieutenant Frank H. Schofield, commanding the U.S.S. *Supply*, reported that he and his crew on February 24, 1904, had clearly viewed three enormous luminous objects moving in unison across the night sky, far at sea in the Atlantic, with the largest of them having a diameter six times that of the sun.

In like vein the journal of the *Royal Astronomical Society of Canada* (March 1913) carried a compilation of reports by Professor Chant of Toronto about unidentified flying objects crossing east to west along the U.S.-Canadian border at a time that subsequent checks revealed no "human" airships had been aloft that night. The reports, gathered from a great number of observers along the route, agreed that a huge luminous body traveled straight across the sky, that the "body was composed of three or four parts with a tail to each part" and as it disappeared a second and third grouping followed. "There were probably thirty or thirty-two such bodies during the period of an hour . . . they moved in fours, threes, and twos, abreast of one another. So perfect was this line-up that it seemed almost as if an aerial fleet were maneuvering. . . ."

There were other reports of UFOs prior to 1947 but they were relatively few compared to the many thousands that have since found their way into the world press, radio, and television. (There are reported to be 10,000 pages of classified UFO documents in CIA headquarters alone.) The increasing flood of these reports points up a pertinent fact: The frequency of UFO sightings increases in direct proportion to our scientific and technological development. Radar installations which detect UFOs are an additional check to visual observations, while increasing numbers of plane flights bring pilots and sometimes passengers into startling proximity to unidentified flying objects, and astronauts frequently encounter them in space, all of which are comparatively recent developments.

Nevertheless, extreme interest in UFOs is still considered something of an aberration, possibly because no concrete proof of any such craft is known to have been found or identified as such. In effect there is no corpus delecti.

If there were and if it had been found in territory controlled by any of the great powers or even of some of the lesser powers it would, quite understandably, have been covered up until the national authorities in question decided what to do about it or how to make it serve their own interests and purposes.

This is possibly the explanation of the Roswell Incident. However, far from being just an interesting mystery, one that has had its day in the press and then subsided, the Roswell Incident is still going on. According to reports, the remains of the craft are still being studied (perhaps with a view to duplication), research is continuing on the composition of the unfamiliar metallic (and other) portions of the space vehicle, unidentifiable hieroglyphic figures reportedly discovered on the interior controls are being subject to computer breakdown, and the cell and internal structure of the humanoid though alien crew members is still undergoing medical analysis. From a public-interest point of view, new statements from witnesses, and the families of witnesses who were previously unwilling to make statements, and "afterthoughts" from some of the military personnel involved in the cover-up present in the following pages rather convincing proof that this crash of a space ship was definitely not a mass delusion but an actual event.

Since the space age began it has often been suggested that we of the human race of earth are on the brink of making contact with some of our neighbors in the cosmos and obtaining final proof that ours is not the only life form in our galaxy. Perhaps this already happened in New Mexico in 1947 and only now, with the discovery of new information and the eventual help of the Freedom of Information Act, will the consequences become apparent.

1

UFOs in the Sky
and in Space

UFOs were really never new. Throughout history, whenever men watched the heavens, they saw or believed they saw flying figures, signs, portents, gods, angels, devils, ships, and, in recent times, having lost an earlier faith, they have seen types of aircraft that apparently come from no earthly base. We have no way of calculating how many of these visions have been caused by misinterpretation or a productive imagination. However, if even 20 percent of these sightings are without earthly explanation, as has been suggested by the data in Air Force Project Blue Book, Special Report No. 14, then there must have been millions of unexplained visitors to the skies of earth since the human species first began to record their impressions of celestial visitors.

In ancient and medieval times portents and objects in the sky were taken more or less as a matter of fact, perhaps because there was no known human air traffic at the time with which to confuse them. From ancient Egypt we have a record that describes huge fiery circles coming from the evening sky, menacing Pharaoh as he stood in a chariot at the head of his army, maintaining throughout the incident, however, a commendable though puzzled *sang-froid*. The prophet Ezekiel may have had dealings with one and with its captain, whom he believed to be the Lord. A reading of the Book of Ezekiel contains an excellent description of the landing of a space capsule, described in simple and understandable language. The ancient skies seemed to be filled with aerial travelers. The Assyrians saw flying bulls, ancient Greeks and Arabs saw flying horses, the opulent Persians thought they saw flying carpets, the warlike Romans watched flying shields and spears and whole battles in the sky at the very moment that they themselves were engaged in earthly combat.

As the ancient world became Christianized, the aerial sightings became fiery crosses and other threatening signs of doom foretelling plagues and disasters. The Emperor Constantine of Byzantium saw something in the sky before a battle that convinced him to become a Christian, considerably changing thereby the course of history.

When the Renaissance opened up people's minds to the exploration of the world, UFOs appropriately took the forms of galleys and caravels, and then, as the French first began experimenting with balloons, certain vast globes were seen floating in the upper heavens, almost as monstrous reflections of what the French were doing. Starting in the late 1800s, relatively modern observers have described UFOs as flying spindles, cigars, and then airships moving at tremendous speeds. In World Wars I and II they were taken to be some sort of unexplained weapon (World War II: "foo fighters") which each side thought the other was using, and it was not until 1947 that the greatly increased number of UFO sightings (at first described as metallic discs or pie pans) were given the name of "flying saucers."

It is possible that all these sightings throughout history, and to an increasing extent in the present, are all versions of the same phenomenon, aided perhaps by imagination and a penchant for seeing what one expects to see. This is why the Chinese have long thought that they have seen hurtling and luminous dragons; the ancient Hindus, two- and three-decked aerial chariots; the Indians of the Americas, great canoes; and tribes and nations in all parts of the earth, luminous monsters, demons, and gods.

But we cannot predicate a mass delusion, especially in a world where many heads of state among the developed nations as well as the highest officials of the United Nations, leading scientists, astronomers, and by now the majority of the earth's population are convinced that we are regularly being visited by UFOs. They appear over large cities, seen by hundreds of thousands. They land near TV stations and power plants and are suspected of having caused the great power blackout of 1965. They buzz passenger planes and are reported to have destroyed military ones. They regularly haunt our advanced research and space-shot centers and follow our capsules into the cosmos. So convinced are large numbers of people about the hovering presence of UFOs that an airfield in France is permanently reserved for their landing, its blue landing lights an invitation only to landing craft not of this earth.

With the breaking of the space barrier it appears that astronauts from earth have begun to meet UFOs in space. If we consider reports that the majority of space ventures have encountered UFOs then the percentage of encounters is vastly greater in space than in the skies of earth. This would seem definitely to indicate that UFOs are of extra-terrestrial origin and, far from being supernatural, are possibly space probes, patrols, or other activity frequently pointed in the direction of earth, an activity antedating our own space efforts over a period of thousands or even millions of years.

While much has been written about UFO sightings and encounters on earth, little has been openly written about encounters with UFOs in space exploration. A rather convincing indication of the presence of UFOs in earth space (but how far out do our space boundaries extend?) has been furnished by mathematician, physicist, and author Maurice Chatelain, a designer of the Apollo spacecraft and former chief of the NASA Communications for the Apollo lunar missions and an outspoken documentalist of one special phase of close encounters in space by explorers (U.S.) from earth with entities from elsewhere. According to Chatelain's accounts, some of which are based on information picked up from "inside sources" while working for NASA in the 1960s, and other relying on data passed on to him later by friends and former colleagues, reports of these encounters made during flights in space have generally been censored, altered, de-emphasized, or simply ignored by NASA and therefore never reached the public at the time of their occurrence. The fact that the astronauts were on military duty was, according to Chatelain, a great and perhaps planned advantage for secrecy inasmuch as they could simply be ordered not to discuss aspects of their UFO encounters. Although the majority of U.S. astronauts are no longer on active duty, they have steadfastly maintained a discreet silence on this topic right up to the present day, leaving us with only Chatelain's "inside" accounts to hint at what might really have gone on in space and even over the surface of the moon. These, to say the least, are visibly impressive.

The following table is detailed in chronological order:

SPACECRAFT/ DATE	CREW	INCIDENT REGARDING UFO OR UNIDENTIFIED SPACE OBJECT
MERCURY May 16, 1963	Cooper	Over Hawaii picked up voices on special frequency speaking in language later examined on tape and found to belong to no known earth language. Passing over Perth, Australia, saw large UFO also observed by checking station on earth.
GEMINI 4 June 3, 1964	McDivitt-White	Over Hawaii almost collided with silver cylinder, oval with luminous trail. Photographed it.
GEMINI 7 December 4, 1965	Borman-Lovell	Took pictures of enormous UFO with propulsion systems following capsule.
GEMINI 9 June 3, 1966	Stafford-Cernan	Capsule accompanied from take-off by many UFOs seen by ground personnel as well as by capsule crew.
GEMINI 10 July 18, 1966	Young-Collins	Two UFOs followed and disappeared when capsule asked ground station for radar observation. Later a huge object not a planet or planetoid was observed.

SPACECRAFT/ DATE	CREW	INCIDENT REGARDING UFO OR UNIDENTIFIED SPACE OBJECT
GEMINI 11 September 12, 1966	Gordon-Conrad	Long object sighted over Madagascar. NASA said it was Soviet Proton 3 but latter was 350 miles away at time of sighting.
APOLLO 8 December 21, 1968	Borman-Lovell-Anders	Sighted disc-shaped UFOs as capsule circled moon. Reported: "We have been informed that Santa Claus does exist." Also picked up unidentifiable language on space-frequency radio.
APOLLO 10 May 18–26, 1969	Stafford-Young-Cernan	Sighted two UFOs following capsule during orbit of moon and homeward flight.
APOLLO 12 November 14, 1969	Conrad-Gordon-Bean	Observatories on earth observed capsule being accompanied by two brilliant UFOs near moon. Then, when near earth before landing, large UFO with red lights was observed.
APOLLO 17 December 7–19, 1972	Cernan-Evans-Schmitt	Saw UFOs near earth, close to moon, and in between.

Although several of the astronauts have flatly denied experiencing UFO sightings in space, and NASA is reported to have dismissed one of its employees for allegedly selling "falsified tape recordings" of conversations similar to the one above, Chatelain maintains that his information is of the most reliable sort and has published this information in his books in France, England, and the United States. (See Bibliography) In his words: "All Apollo or Gemini flights were followed, both at a distance and sometimes . . . quite closely, by space vehicles of extraterrestrial origin. Every time it occurred, the astronauts informed Mission Control, who then ordered absolute silence."

And, of course, these sightings do not include Russian sightings and alleged observations by both Russian and American astronauts of ruins, constructions, and "pyramids" on the moon which may or may not have bearings on present UFO activity. It indicates, however, a lively curiosity in our own space activities on the part of entities unknown. Besides these meetings in the cosmos there are sightings, close and distant, by thousands of chance observers on earth as they watch the skies by night or by day. There are persistent though difficult-to-verify reports of cosmic kidnapings wherein startled human beings have been taken aboard UFOs, kept there, questioned, brainwashed, and then released, generally with memory and especially time lapses, because of which what seemed a few minutes to them has been several days in earth time. Disappearances of people in isolated locations, unexplained deaths, and draining of blood from animals have frequently been blamed on UFOs—a convenient target—as if they were scouting the earth like a gigantic game preserve for food or specimens.

In spite of the ubiquity and frequency of UFO sightings and alleged encounters, as of this moment there is no concrete evidence available that they exist and that they are not in some way natural phenomena, as for example, glowing swamp gas, refractions of starlight, swarms of insects that generate electricity, or visual retention of the image of the moon or of stars—rather imaginative explanations, themselves worthy of some of the more picturesque UFO reports. Also, many of the more carefully documented UFO "encounter" reports come from ranchers, truck drivers, state troopers, sheriffs, and others whose duties normally take them out into the lonely spaces of night. (The incidents in the film *Close Encounters of the Third Kind* were based on reported UFO happenings.) But if extraterrestrials on board UFOs wished to make contact with the human race, why would they select relatively unimportant individuals instead of landing at the seats of power, such as in the center court of the Pentagon, in the middle of Red Square, or in front of the Tien-an-men Gate, for more direct summit conversations?

It is of course natural for scientists, and especially for astronomers, to exercise an understandable caution in approaching a subject which, however popular, remains devoid of positive acceptance. One astronomer (nameless of course) quoted in Dr. Peter Sturrock's *Report on Survey of the Membership of the American Astronomers Society Concerning the UFO Problem* (Stanford, 1975) speaks for the majority: " . . . I find it tough to make a living as an astronomer these days. It would be professionally suicidal to devote significant time to UFOs. . . ."

Throughout the world, as far as is available to public knowledge, no definite proof exists that UFOs are a product of individual or mass hypnotism. Even though we know that pilots have disappeared or died while chasing or being chased by a UFO they are still presumed by most scientists and astronomers to have been victims of their own imaginations.

Just suppose, however, that one of these "imaginary" UFOs made a crash landing at a place that could be reached by Air Force or other investigative teams. Suppose, moreover, that it would be in sufficient repair to be identified as a UFO and would contain fairly intact though dead humanoid extraterrestrials within the capsule. There would be indications of writing on the control panel and on a parchment-like substance scattered around, and the writing would later prove to be of no earthly language. If this happened, it would considerably strengthen the belief in extraterrestrial life and advanced technology but, at the same time, present the government of the country where it landed with a problem of how to deal with the happening—whether to share it (with the possible secret of its operation) with the world or to deny that it ever happened.

A number of elements in the above science-fiction scenario were rather convincingly carried out in New Mexico some years ago. The first scene could be titled as follows:

PLACE: The teletype room of Radio KOAT, Albuquerque, New Mexico.
TIME: July 7, 1947, at four o'clock in the afternoon.

2

Incident at Roswell

Lydia Sleppy, who, in addition to her other office and administrative duties for radio station KOAT in Albuquerque, New Mexico, was also the teletype operator, was sitting at her machine at the station at approximately 4 P.M. The date was July 7, 1947. Suddenly the phone rang with a message that would affect news reports for the next few days throughout the world, and whose import may not yet be fully apparent. The call was from Johnny McBoyle, reporter and part owner of sister station KSWS in Roswell, New Mexico—a station which had no teletype of its own but which frequently used the KOAT machine when it had something to report. This time his voice was excited:

"Lydia, get ready for a scoop! We want to get this on the ABC wire right away. Listen to this! A flying saucer has crashed . . . No, I'm not joking. It crashed near Roswell. I've been there and seen it. It's like a big crumpled dishpan. Some rancher has hauled it under a cattle shelter with his tractor. The Army is there and they are going to pick it up. The whole area is now closed off. And get this—they're saying something about little men being on board. . . . Start getting this on the teletype right away while I'm on the phone.''

Understandably bemused, Lydia placed the phone in the uncomfortable position between ear and shoulder and started to type McBoyle's startling statements into the teletype. But after she had typed only several sentences the machine suddenly stopped itself. As this is a common occurrence with teletypes for a variety of reasons, Lydia was not concerned, although she had never been cut off the air before in the middle of a transmission. Moving the telephone from her neck to her hand, she informed McBoyle that the teletype had stopped at her end.

This time, according to her recollections, he seemed not only excited but under pressure and apparently speaking to someone else at the same time. His voice seemed strained. ''Wait a minute, I'll get back to you. . . . Wait. . . . I'll get right back.'' But he did not. Instead the teletype went on again by itself and started addressing Albuquerque, or Lydia, directly. The sender was not identified and the tone was formal and curt: ATTENTION ALBUQUERQUE: DO NOT TRANSMIT. REPEAT DO NOT TRANSMIT THIS MESSAGE. STOP COMMUNICATION IMMEDIATELY.

As Lydia still had McBoyle on the phone she told him what had just come over the teletype and asked: ''What do I do now?''

His reply was unexpected. ''Forget about it. You never heard it. Look, you're not supposed to know. Don't talk about it to anyone.''

(McBoyle later told Lydia Sleppy that he had witnessed a plane, which he said was destined for Wright Field— Wright-Patterson—take off with the object or parts of it on board, but was unable to get anywhere near it because of the tight security maintained by heavily armed guards.)

Although this was Lydia's last connection with the "happening" she had ample time for subsequent reflection about it, since it was to become a topic of considerable discussion after the return of her boss, Merle Tucker, who had been out of town at the time of the occurrence. Tucker was concerned that his station's involvement in the incident could jeopardize his recent application for an FCC license for a subsidiary station he was preparing to add to his Rio Grande Broadcasting Network. What particularly bothered him was that, try as he could, he was totally unable to verify that the incident had actually taken place.

Especially interesting, however, is that many of the people he tried to talk to about it insisted that the object had come down in the area west of Socorro, New Mexico, rather than near Roswell, and that a sheriff's deputy from that town had been to the spot and had viewed the wreckage of some sort of saucer-shaped object along with a small burned patch of ground. "Then all of a sudden," he recalled in a recent interview, "we couldn't find anything or anyone who would talk about it." Tucker himself, while he vividly recalled the incident, was reluctant to be interviewed about the matter, and absolutely refused to allow the interview to be taped. Nuclear physicist and researcher Stanton T. Friedman met with a similar wall of silence when he located and tried to interview McBoyle on the same topic. McBoyle's reaction: "Forget about it. . . . It never happened."

It probably occurred to Lydia, as it did to other area residents and investigators, that the incident was most likely concerned with the reported presence of "flying saucers" (not yet referred to as UFOs) which seemed to be operating in force in the area of New Mexico and Arizona during June and July 1947. This was, incidentally, relatively close in time to the June 24 sighting of the famous flight of nine "pie pans" over Mount Rainier, Washington, by Kenneth Arnold—a spectacular sighting which initiated the first intensive public interest in UFOs and led to the general use of the term *flying saucers* to describe them.

These subsequent reports indicated a swirling UFO activity by night and by day in Arizona and New Mexico—an activity easily justified by the fact that in the late 1940s New Mexico was the site of the major portion of America's postwar defense efforts in atomic research, rocketry, aircraft and missile development, and radar-electronics experimentation. Los Alamos, the sprawling scientific community created by the Manhattan Project in 1943 especially to provide the manpower and facilities necessary for the wartime construction and testing of the world's first atomic bombs, was still a "secret city" in 1947—a highly restricted area. Of similar status was the White Sands Missile Range and Proving Grounds around Alamogordo, where top-level research was being carried out on the only captured German V-2 rockets in existence on our side of the Iron Curtain. Also stationed in New Mexico, at Roswell, was the only combat-trained atom-bomb group in the world at that time—the 509th Bomb Group of the U.S. Army Air Force. All of which makes it somewhat easier to understand why, in those summer months of 1947, New Mexico experienced more UFO sightings both per capita and per square mile than any other state in the union. Certainly alien intelligences systematically engaged in the observation of this planet and its civilization could be expected to concentrate their efforts on monitoring those areas exhibiting the highest levels of scientific and technological activity.

The following reports are not only typical but are of special interest because of the sighters' ability to describe the shape (difficult to do, especially by night) of what they saw:

JUNE 25, 1947: A saucer-shaped object about one half the size of the full moon was reported moving south over Silver City, New Mexico, by the local dentist, Dr. R. F. Sensenbaugher.

JUNE 26, 1947: Leon Oetinger, M.D., of Lexington, Kentucky, and three other witnesses reported a large, silver, ball-shaped object—clearly not a balloon or a dirigible—traveling at high speed near the edge of the Grand Canyon.

JUNE 27, 1947: John A. Petsche, an electrician at Phelps-Dodge Corporation, and other witnesses reported a disc-shaped object overhead and apparently coming to earth about 10:30 A.M. near Tintown in the vicinity of Bisbee in southeastern Arizona near the New Mexico border.

JUNE 27, 1947: Major George B. Wilcox of Warren, Arizona, reported a series of eight or nine perfectly spaced discs traveling at high speed with a wobbling motion. He said the discs passed over his house at three-second intervals heading east, and estimated them to be at a height of about 1,000 feet above the mountaintops.

JUNE 27, 1947: A "white disc glowing like an electric light bulb" was reported to have passed over Pope, New Mexico, by local resident W. C. Dobbs at 9:50 A.M. Minutes later, the same or a similar object was sighted traveling southwest over the White Sands Missile Range by Captain E. B. Detchmendy, who reported it to his commanding officer, Lieutenant Colonel Harold R. Turner. At

10:00 A.M. Mrs. David Appelzoller of San Miguel, New Mexico, reported that a similar object had passed over that city, again heading southwest. Colonel Turner of White Sands initially reacted by announcing that no rockets had been launched from that base since June 12. Later, fearing hysteria, he officially "identified" the object as a "daytime meteorite" *(sic)*.

JUNE 28, 1947: Captain F. Dvyn, a pilot flying in the vicinity of Alamogordo, New Mexico, witnessed "a ball of fire with a fiery blue trail behind it" *pass beneath* his aircraft and appear to disintegrate while he watched.

JUNE 29, 1947: Army Air Force pilots conducted a search for an object reported to have fallen near Cliff, New Mexico, sometime in the forenoon, but find nothing but a curious odor in the air.

JUNE 29, 1947: A team of naval rocket-test experts headed by Dr. C. J. Zohn, on duty at the White Sands Proving Grounds, watched a silvery-colored disc do a series of maneuvers at high altitude over the secret rocket-test range.

JUNE 30, 1947: Thirteen silvery disc-shaped objects were observed by a railroad worker named Price traveling one after another over Albuquerque, New Mexico. Initially heading south, they changed course abruptly to east, and then reversed dramatically to west before disappearing. Price alerted his neighbors, and the entire neighborhood rushed out of their houses to lie on their lawns and observe the maneuvers in the sky above them.

JUNE 30, 1947 (as reported from the Tucumcari [New Mexico] *Daily News* on July 9): "Mrs. Helen Hardin, employee of Quay County Abstract Co., reported

Tuesday, July 8, that she saw a flying saucer from her front porch about 11 P.M. June 30 traveling from east to west at high speed. She said it looked to be about half the size of the full moon with a slight yellow cast. She watched it for about six seconds, low in the sky and going down outside of town rather than close in. She at first thought it was a meteor but noticed a whirling motion as it neared the ground. Also it was not falling as fast as meteors do.''

JULY 1, 1947: Max Hood, an executive of the Albuquerque Chamber of Commerce, reported seeing a bluish disc zigzagging across the northwestern sky over Albuquerque.

JULY 1–6, 1947: Seven separate reports of flying discs over northern Mexico ranging from Mexicali to Juárez.

JULY 1, 1947: Mr. and Mrs. Frank Munn reported witnessing a large object moving east over Phoenix about 9:00 P.M.

JULY 2, 1947: Mr. and Mrs. Dan Wilmot of Roswell, New Mexico, witnessed a large, glowing object as it passed over their house traveling northwest at a high rate of speed. (See Chapter 3)

What were these people seeing? Certainly not tests of the high-flying V-2 model rockets being flown from White Sands at the time, as some skeptics have suggested. A check of the White Sands records shows that the only V-2 tests conducted anywhere near the time frame in question were one on June 12 and another on July 3.

It would be easy to suggest that these sightings, coming after the well-publicized Mount Rainier reports, were auto-induced optical suggestions by witnesses as they examined the skies for flying objects like the ones discussed in the press from this time onward, the observers having a tendency to consider any cloud, bird, or reflection to be a UFO. This has generally been the normal official reaction to UFO reports and this is a contributing factor to the estimate that thousands of UFO sightings go unreported annually and will continue to do so unless some concrete evidence is found and made public, either of a real UFO or a living or dead example of extraterrestrial life.

It is interesting to consider that, at the very beginning of the 1947 UFO flap, and attested to by witnesses, press releases, interviews, radio reports, and uninhibited by censorship that came too late, the Army Air Force came into possession of a bona-fide UFO together with the remains of its crew. And apparently since that time the Air Force and the United States Government have been trying to decide what to do with it.

3

The AAF Confronts a Crashed UFO and Dead Extraterrestrials

At about ten minutes to ten on the evening of July 2, 1947, local hardware dealer Dan Wilmot and his wife were sitting on the front porch of their South Penn Street home in Roswell, New Mexico, enjoying a cool respite from what had been one of those hot New Mexico summer days. In Wilmot's words, "All of a sudden a big glowing object zoomed out of the sky from the southeast. It was going northwest [toward Corona, New Mexico] at a high rate of speed."

Somewhat startled, Wilmot and his wife ran out into their yard to watch as an oval object shaped "like two inverted saucers faced mouth to mouth," and glowing as if lit from the inside, passed over their house and out of sight to the northwest in forty to fifty seconds. Although Wilmot described the mysterious object as having been completely silent, Mrs. Wilmot later said she thought she had heard a slight swishing sound for a brief moment as the object passed overhead.

Concerned that he might be leaving himself open to

ridicule, Wilmot, described by the Roswell *Daily Record* as "one of the most respected and reliable citizens in town," kept silent about his experience for nearly a week in hopes that "someone else would come out and tell about having seen one."

But nobody told Wilmot anything that might corroborate his experience until, on July 8, an unusual release to the press came from the public information officer at the Roswell base. In view of the ensuing excitement, it may have occurred later to Wilmot that he had seen a preview of an incident which later developed into a well-kept and continuing secret, at least as far as the public was concerned. It was not treated as such when it first happened.

On July 8, one day after Mrs. Sleppy's unusual incident with the TWX teletype machine, Lieutenant Walter Haut, public information officer at the Roswell Army Air Base, acting on information beginning to filter in to the Roswell Air Base, jumped the gun in a burst of excitement and enthusiastically issued the following release to members of the press without first bothering to obtain the authorization of his base commander, Colonel William Blanchard—an oversight he was to be made painfully aware of later:

> Roswell Army Air Base, Roswell, N.M.
> 8th July, 1947, A.M.

> The many rumors regarding the flying disc became a reality yesterday when the intelligence office of the 509th Bomb Group of the Eighth Air Force, Roswell Army Air Field, was fortunate enough to gain possession of a disc through the cooperation of one of the local ranchers and the sheriff's office of Chaves County.
> The flying object landed on a ranch near Roswell sometime last week. Not having phone facilities, the

Roswell Army Air Base Public Information Officer First Lieutenant Walter G. Haut, the man responsible for the release of the so-called "Roswell Statement," which announced that the U.S. Army Air Force had recovered the remains of a crashed UFO. According to several press sources, Haut was later hushed up by "several blistering phone calls from Washington."

(RAAF Yearbook, 1947, courtesy Walter Haut)

rancher stored the disc until such time as he was able to contact the sheriff's office, who in turn notified Major Jesse A. Marcel of the 509th Bomb Group Intelligence Office.

Action was immediately taken and the disc was

ROSWELL STATEMENT

Here is the unqualified statement issued by the Roswell Army Base public relations officer:

"The many rumors regarding the flying disc became a reality yesterday when the intelligence office of the 509th Bomb Group of the Eighth Air Force, Roswell Army Air Field, was fortunate enough to gain possession of a disc through the co-operation of one of the local ranchers and the Sheriff's office of Chaves county.

"The flying object landed on a ranch near Roswell sometime last week. Not having phone facilities, the rancher stored the disc until such time as he was able to contact the Sheriff's office, who in turn notified Major Jesse A. Marcel, of the 509th Bomb Group Intelligence office.

"Action was immediately taken and the disc was picked up at the rancher's home. It was inspected at the Roswell Army Air Field and subsequently loaned by Major Marcel to higher headquarters."

The text of the July 8, 1947 "Roswell Statement" issued to the press by First Lieutenant Haut.

(San Francisco Chronicle, *7-9-47)*

picked up at the rancher's home. It was inspected at the Roswell Army Air Field and subsequently loaned by Major Marcel to higher headquarters.

This release, which was enthusiastically picked up by the Associated Press and the New York *Times* wire service and others, managed to appear in numerous newspapers across the United States, as well as in a number of foreign journals, including the prestigious London *Times*.

The day before the release from the army base, an AP release went out over the wire service datelined San Francisco, July 7, under the headline: FLYING SAUCERS SEEN IN MOST STATES NOW. Dealing with a phenomenal increase in UFO sightings in the United States during the previous two weeks, it almost served as an introduction to the incident which would attain worldwide prominence the next day.

The Roswell *Daily Record* rushed into print on July 8 with the following report, captioned RAAF CAPTURES FLYING SAUCER IN ROSWELL REGION. NO DETAILS OF FLYING DISCS ARE REVEALED. The following article implied both a solution of the Flying Saucer Controversy and a suggestion that the AAF was already involved in the beginnings of cover-ups. Pertinent points of the article follow:

The Intelligence Office of the 509th Bombardment group at Roswell Army Air Field announced at noon today that the field has come into possession of a flying saucer.

According to information released by the department, over authority of Major J. A. Marcel, intelligence officer, the disc was recovered on a ranch in the Roswell vicinity after an unidentified rancher had notified Sheriff George Wilcox, here, that he had found the instrument on his premises.

Major Marcel and a detail from his department went to the ranch and recovered the disc, it was stated.

After the intelligence office here had inspected the

Front page of the Roswell *Daily Record* for Tuesday, July 8, 1947. *(Roswell* Daily Record, *Jack Swickard, editor)*

instrument it was flown (by aircraft) to "higher headquarters."

The intelligence office stated that no details of the saucer's construction or its appearance had been revealed.

Another article in the same July 8 issue of the Roswell *Daily Record* reported that the operator and pilots of a private airfield at Carrizozo (about thirty-five miles south-west of the Brazel crash site) claimed to have seen a similar object in flight. According to the article:

Mark Sloan, operator of the Carrizozo flying field, reported a flying saucer sped over the field at about a 4,000- to 6,000-foot altitude.

Sloan said the phenomenon was observed by himself, Grady Warren, flying instructor, and Nolan Lovelace, Ray Shafer, and another man, all pilots. He made this description:

"When we first noticed it about 10:00 A.M. we thought it resembled a feather because it was oscillating. Then we noticed its great speed and decided it was a flying saucer. Our guesses are that it was moving at between 200 and 600 miles per hour.

"It passed over the field and almost directly up from southwest to northwest and was in sight in all only about ten seconds."

It could, of course, be suspected that Sloan had "latched on" to the incident to give some publicity to his flying field. But later it was to appear that numerous other witnesses had heard or seen something very unusual in the sky over Roswell around the time of the landing of a still-unidentified flying object.

Perhaps the weather had something to do with the sightings and the alleged crash. Some seventy-five miles to the northwest, one of the worst lightning storms to strike the area in a long time was beginning to rage over the bleak New Mexico landscape. Lightning storms had occasionally brought down aircraft in the past.

The sketchy information used by Lieutenant Haut to write his initial news release was hardly sufficient to supply the press with certain additional details of possibly crucial importance which numerous other witnesses, including ranchers, soldiers, a civil engineer, a group of student archaeologists, and law enforcement officers, had observed at two distinctly different sites within the area that were apparently connected with the same crash. These reputedly included a large flying saucer and the remains of half a dozen or so humanoid creatures, pale in skin coloring, about four feet tall, and dressed in a kind of one-piece jump-suit uniform. Nor did they mention a great quantity of highly unusual wreckage, much of it metallic in nature, apparently originating from the same object and described by Major Marcel as "nothing made on this earth." Neither was any mention made to the press of later information reported by witnesses concerning certain columns of hieroglyphic-like writing or recording on a wooden-like substance (that was not wood) and similar unknown lettering on the control panels of the disc or saucer.

That Lieutenant Haut had ample opportunity to regret even the small amount of information he had given out is now evident. Almost immediately a news blackout descended over Roswell while higher authorities as far away as the Pentagon decided what the next move would be.

Several hours later, a new bit of information was suddenly released. It now appeared that the object was merely a crashed weather balloon. Most papers copied this new information, with the notable exception of the Washington *Post*, which referred rather pointedly to a "news blackout."

Meanwhile, Brigadier General Roger M. Ramey, commander of the Eighth Air Force District at Fort Worth, was alerted by a phone call from Lieutenant General Hoyt Vandenberg, Deputy Chief of the Air Force, that pieces of

View of the runway at Roswell Army Air Base as it looked in 1947.

(RAAF Yearbook, 1947, courtesy Walter Haut)

the object were on the Roswell Air Base (now called the
Walker Air Force Base). General Ramey at once called
Colonel Blanchard and made known his extreme displea-
sure as well as that of General Vandenberg for Blanchard's
having initiated the press release. He then directed that the
Roswell portion of the wreckage be immediately loaded
aboard a B-29. With two generals ''breathing down his
neck,'' Colonel Blanchard lost no time in ordering Major
Marcel personally to fly this material to the general's
headquarters at Carswell Air Force Base, Fort Worth,
Texas, for his examination before flying it on to Wright-
Patterson Field in Dayton, Ohio, where it would undergo
the ''further analysis'' prescribed for it by General Vandenberg himself.

Ramey then went on the air on a hook-up hastily patched
out of a Fort Worth radio station to nervously assure the
public that the crashed ''fl-fly-fling disc'' was really nothing more than the remains of a downed weather balloon,

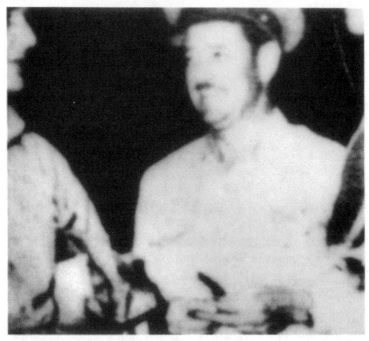

Brigadier General Roger Maxwell Ramey, Commander, 8th Air Force, at Roswell Air Base in 1947. Records show that Ramey paid what is described only as "an official visit" to the Roswell Base on the night of July 16/17, 1947, barely a week after the flying disc recovery story hit the newswires.

(RAAF Yearbook, 1947, courtesy Walter Haut)

and that the whole thing was due only to a case of mistaken identity. "There is no such gadget [as a flying disc] known to the Army," he said somberly, and then hastily added the qualification, "at least not at this level."

After the broadcast, in response to a question from a group of still skeptical Fort Worth press reporters about where the remains of the alleged "weather device" were at that moment, Ramey snapped irritably, "It's in my office, and it will probably stay right there!" He then repeated for the reporters what he had just said on the air:

"The special flight to Wright Field has been canceled, gentlemen. This whole affair has been most unfortunate, but in light of the excitement that has been stirred up lately about these so-called flying discs, it is not surprising. Now let's all go home and call it an evening."

While some members of the press may have suspected that Ramey was shading the truth, they had no proof. However, an interesting comment on this incident was supplied during a September 9, 1979, interview with General Ramey's former adjutant, Colonel Thomas Jefferson DuBose, now a retired brigadier general. Speaking from a comfortable margin of thirty-two years after the event, he observed that there had been received "orders from on high to ship the material from Roswell directly to Wright Field by special plane." He added that the general (Ramey) was in complete charge and the rest of the officers and men involved "just followed orders." The general was most concerned that the large number of press reporters present be "taken off his back in a hurry." The weather balloon story was a fabrication designed to accomplish that task and "put out the fire" at the same time. He did not recall who first suggested the weather-balloon explanation, but thinks it may have been Ramey himself.

Colonel (now General) DuBose is the man pictured with Ramey on page 32 posing for reporters on the floor of Ramey's office with the hastily substituted wreckage of a real Rawin weather balloon. Only nine months later, in May of 1948, DuBose was to become chief of staff of the Eighth Air Force at Fort Worth.

A striking example of how command can orchestrate new policy with original reports, even if it entails a certain modification of what has been reported, is afforded by the case of Warrant Officer Irving Newton. At the time of the Roswell Incident, Newton was in charge of the Base Weather

Fort Worth Army Air Base, July 8, 1947. Less than twenty-four hours after the Army Air Force announced that it had recovered the wreckage of a crashed UFO on a New Mexico ranch, it permitted the release of the photo on the left to back up its claim that the debris was only parts of a downed weather balloon. "Actually," said Major Jesse Marcel, shown kneeling here amid what he described as some of the less spectacular pieces of wreckage, "this material may have *looked* like tinfoil and balsa wood, but the resemblance ended there." At first newsmen were permitted only as close to this material as was necessary to take the picture. Later, after torn-up pieces of an actual weather device had been substituted for the real wreckage on General Ramey's orders, press photographers were permitted to photograph and examine at will. The photo on the right, which was widely published in the press the next day, shows General Ramey and his adjutant Colonel DuBose posing with this substitute "wreckage" at the very moment that the real wreckage was en route to Wright Field for scientific examination.

(Fort Worth Star-Telegram)

Office and Flight Services at the Carswell-Fort Worth Air Base in Texas.

As Newton recollects, he had neither seen nor heard anything about the Roswell Incident on July 7. But on the night of July 8, as he was working in the Weather Office, the phone rang. It was General Ramey. The general ordered Newton to report to his office immediately. Newton, in spite of a certain urgency in the general's tone, nevertheless found the courage to inform the general that he was the only man on duty in the Weather Office and as such he was also in charge of flight-control operations that evening. To Newton's mildly couched protest the general replied with a decisive command flair: "Get your ass over here in ten minutes. If you can't get a car commandeer the first one that comes along—on my orders."

When Newton got to his destination he was briefed by a colonel to the effect that an object had been found by a major in Roswell and that the general had decided that it was really a weather balloon and wanted him (Newton) to identify it as such. After this hurried briefing Newton was ushered into a room filled with reporters and photographers where he was handed several pieces of what he immediately recognized as material belonging to a Rawin-type balloon, although somewhat "deteriorated." A number of other pieces were laid out on brown paper on the floor. While the examination was taking place a series of photographs were taken of the general and his aide.

Newton said (Moore interview, July 1979): "It was cut and dried. I had sent up thousands of them and there's no doubt that *what I was given* were parts of a balloon. I was later told that the major from Roswell had identified the stuff as a flying saucer but that the general had been suspicious of this identification from the beginning and that's why I had been called.

A "Rawin target" weather device, 1947, consisting of an extremely light and flimsy foiled-paper radar target attached to a thin balsa wood frame by staples and carried aloft by several helium-filled polyethylene balloons. The total weight was less than two pounds. The Air Force's cover story that the debris found on the Foster ranch had resulted from the crash of one of these was so hastily contrived that the Air Force incorrectly identified it as a "Rawin sonde"—an entirely different device.

(U.S. Meteorological Service)

QUESTION: *But wouldn't the people at Roswell have been able to identify a balloon on their own?*

They certainly should have. It was a regular Rawin sonde. They must have seen hundreds of them.

What happened after your identification of the object?
When I had identified it as a balloon I was dismissed.

Can you describe the fabric? Was it easy to tear?
Certainly. You would have to be careful not to tear it. The metal involved was likely an extremely thin Alcoa wrap. It was very flimsy.

In this connection we note that Major Marcel as well as others were insistent about the great strength of the bits of metallic material they found, how it could not be torn or even dented by sledgehammer blows. It seems fairly evident that the wreckage did not, in spite of official second thoughts, come from a Rawin balloon.

Another telling error on the part of Ramey's office can be found in the initial news releases identifying the Roswell wreckage as having come from a balloon. It is important to note here that in 1947 there were two distinct types of Rawin devices in use—the Rawin target (ML-306) and the Rawin sonde (AN/AMT-4). As Newton, and certainly any other competent weather officer of the time, would have known, only one of these, the Rawin target, incorporated metallic foil as part of its design. The Rawin sonde consisted only of a 100-200 gram *neoprene* balloon attached to a small radio transmitter. Yet the news release from Ramey's office, which was clearly written *before* Newton's examination of the device (note that the photo of Ramey on page 32 shows him holding a copy of that very document), appears ignorant of this all-important fact and identifies the wreckage as "debris from a Rawin sonde." The error was later corrected in subsequent releases but appears to have escaped the attention of the press.

The balloon story may even have been inspired by an event that had occurred only three days earlier on a farm in

A "Rawin sonde" weather device in flight over New Mexico. These devices usually consist of an 18" x 10" two-pound instrument package suspended from a polyethylene plastic balloon and are used to detect weather conditions at high altitudes. The instrument package attached to these balloons carries a "Notice to Finder" plaque and is readily identifiable if recovered on the ground. The Air Force's initial confusion between the "Rawin sonde" shown here and the "Rawin target" shown on the previous page seems to indicate a hastily concocted story for the benefit of newsmen.

(New Mexico Institute of Mining and Technology, Socorro, New Mexico)

Circleville, Pickway County, Ohio. On July 5, 1947, the tinfoil and paper wreckage of a real Rawin target device was discovered on the ground by Sherman Campbell, a local farmer. It was immediately identified as such by the military without the necessity of first sending it on to "higher headquarters" for examination. A second such device, discovered on July 8 by David C. Heffner, was also quickly identified. In neither case was there anything strange or inexplicable about the wreckage.

Considerable information about the construction and purpose of weather and other scientific-purpose balloons used in the late 1940s was obtained in a series of interviews with C. B. Moore, aerologist and physicist currently with the New Mexico Institute of Mining and Technology at Socorro. In the summer of 1947, Moore (no relation to the author) was directly involved in a New York University-sponsored high-altitude-research balloon project based out of the North Field of White Sands, near Alamogordo, New Mexico, a project which, he said, he believed was responsible for "at least *some* of the flying-saucer reports in the area." Later that winter he took part in the launching of the Navy's first Skyhook upper-atmospheric research balloon from Camp Ripley, near Minneapolis, Minnesota, under the auspices of General Mills. He said:

> The Skyhooks resulted from the Navy's 1946 Project Helios, designed originally to launch human scientists to high altitudes to make scientific measurements. Later it was decided to use instruments instead, and Project Skyhook developed. The project was initially classified "Confidential" just so public information on them could be controlled. The first balloon was constructed of vinyl chloride and was inflated at New Brighton, Minnesota, during the summer of 1947, but

there were no actual launchings until about six months later. The vinyl chloride composition was changed to polyethylene early on—perhaps in January of 1948, and was used up to the end of the project. These balloons could lift a seventy-pound payload. . . . Only a very few of these were ever launched in New Mexico, and none certainly in 1947.

When asked whether the Roswell device might have been a weather or other scientific balloon, Moore replied: "Based on the description you just gave me, I can definitely rule this out. There wasn't a balloon in use back in '47, or even today for that matter, that could have produced debris over such a large area or torn up the ground in any way. I have no idea what such an object might have been, but I can't believe a balloon would fit such a description."

C. B. Moore's description of a Rawin target device, of which he had seen and handled many, was also important in that it strongly reinforced the belief that anyone finding such "flimsy foil and balsa-wood material" would have had great difficulty in confusing it with anything out of the ordinary.

One is compelled to admire the tactics of the headquarters in question as a way of defusing public interest in—or even panic caused by—the incident. If, for example, a blanket denial had been made, it would probably have served only to increase curiosity, but a human admission of a case of mistaken identity, even on the part of the Air Force, induced a certain sympathetic understanding and, more important, deflated the mystery of the incident as surely as letting out the helium would deflate a real weather balloon.

Now, on July 9, a rash of denials appeared in the press.

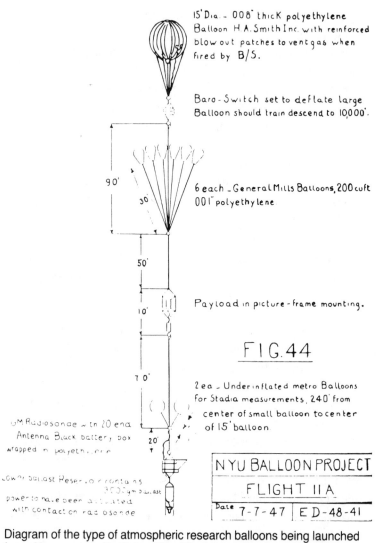

15' Dia. - 008" thick polyethylene Balloon H.A. Smith Inc. with reinforced blow out patches to vent gas when fired by B/S.

Baro-Switch set to deflate large Balloon should train descend to 10,000'.

6 each - General Mills Balloons, 200 cuft 001" polyethylene

90'

30'

50'

Payload in picture-frame mounting.

10'

FIG. 44

7 0'

2 ea - Under inflated metro Balloons for Stadia measurements, 240' from center of small balloon to center of 15' balloon.

GM Radiosonde - tn 20 end Antenna Black battery box wrapped in polyeth...

20'

Lower ballast Reservoir contains ... gm ballast power to have been activated with contact on radiosonde

N Y U BALLOON PROJECT
FLIGHT II A

| Date 7-7-47 | E D-48-41 |

Diagram of the type of atmospheric research balloons being launched from Alamogordo Air Base, New Mexico, at the time of the saucer crash in July 1947. This particular diagram refers to flight 11-A, launched July 7, 1947. Although these balloons were frequently mistaken for UFOs while aloft, it is difficult to imagine how they could be mistaken for one while on the ground.

(U.S. Air Force)

The Dallas *Morning News:* SUSPECTED "DISC"
ONLY FLYING WEATHER VANE

The Daily Times Herald (Dallas): SERVICES TRY
TO STOP "DISC" TALK. The article included
the observation, "Persons who thought they had
their hands on the $3,000 offered for a genuine
flying saucer found their hands full of nothing."

The Roswell *Daily Record* ran an eight-column headline: GENERAL RAMEY EMPTIES ROSWELL
SAUCER, with a subtitle introducing the theme of
the lead article: General Ramey says disc is weather
balloon.

In the same issue, there is a story about a rancher,
William Brazel, who had alerted the sheriff's office at
Roswell about unusual debris that had fallen out of the
sky after an aerial explosion. The story was headlined:
HARASSED RANCHER WHO LOCATED "SAUCER"
SORRY HE TOLD ABOUT IT. Brazel, who throughout
this interview had obviously gone to great pains to tell the
newspaper people exactly what the Air Force had in-
structed him to say regarding how he had come to discover
the wreckage and what it looked like, showed a bit of
independent spirit at the end of the session by risking
the opinion that, regardless of what he had just said,
it was still no weather balloon. He was familiar with
weather balloons from past experiences, he observed, and
"I am sure what I found was not any weather observation
balloon. . . . But if I find anything else besides a bomb,
they are going to have a hard time getting me to say
anything about it."

Although the Roswell paper faithfully printed General
Ramey's balloon story on the first page (as we have already noted), it was clear on the editorial page that they

weren't exactly buying it either. Seeming to sense that what Brazel had said in his interview had apparently been carefully rigged by the Air Force, and surmising, nevertheless, that AAF officers would know a weather balloon when they saw one, the *Record* cautiously editorialized:

AND NOW WHAT IS IT?

With the telephone ringing, excited voices shouting into newsroom personnel ears pouring out eager questions which were unanswerable, it was discovered shortly after publication time of the *Record* yesterday afternoon that curiosity over reports from 44 states of the Union that silver discs had been seen had crystallized into belief.

The *Record* had no more than "hit the street" until the telephone barrage began, with questioners checking up on what they had just read, doubtful of their own eyes.

But the story stood, just as all amazing things stand in these days of wonderful feats and curious performances.

What the disc is is another matter. The Army isn't telling its secrets yet, from all appearances when this was written. Maybe it's a fluke, and maybe it isn't. Anyone's guess is pretty good at the moment.

Maybe the thing is still a hoax, as has been the belief of most folks from the start. But, SOMETHING has been found.

Dealing with the radio broadcast made by General Ramey to further deflate the excitement caused by the first announcement, the San Francisco *Chronicle* added in an archly contrived comment that "The mysterious flying discs have been seen all over the nation (except Kansas which is dry) and have been described as traveling . . . 1,200 miles an hour.''

This last example, a technique of treating UFO reports as being made by persons who were either drunk or eccentric visionaries has, of course, been frequently employed by the media from 1947 on.

Meanwhile, as press reporters continued to try to contact Colonel Blanchard, the colonel suddenly and conveniently went on leave on July 8, 1947, at the very same time that Major Marcel was flying with the crashed debris to Carswell. Command of the base was temporarily assumed by the base deputy commander, Lieutenant Colonel Payne Jennings. When reporters persisted in their attempts to reach Colonel Blanchard, they were informed that "He is on leave and therefore unavailable for comment."

Although there is no doubt that Colonel Blanchard would certainly have followed without question Ramey's orders about how to deal with the alleged flying disc, he would also have possessed sufficient qualifications to have known whether he was dealing with the remains of a weather balloon. Blanchard, who was later destined to attain the rank of three-star general, was, in 1947, already a highly decorated war hero with a distinguished war record as commander of bomb groups in the Pacific and later as operations officer of the Twentieth Air Force. Although few knew it at the time, Blanchard had come within a hair's breadth of being chosen as one of the pilots designated to drop America's first atom bombs on Japan in 1945. He was beaten out in the competition only by the two who actually dropped the bombs.

Although General Blanchard is now dead, his widow recently confirmed (interview with Stanton Friedman) that her husband knew that the wreckage that he had sent to

Lieutenant Colonel Payne Jennings, the man who assumed command of the Roswell Army Air Base on July 8, 1947, after Colonel W. H. Blanchard conveniently "went on leave." Jennings was later lost when his plane mysteriously vanished over the Bermuda Triangle while on a flight to England.

(RAAF Yearbook, 1947, courtesy Walter Haut)

Colonel (later Major General) William H. Blanchard, Commanding Officer, Roswell Army Air Base, 1947. One of Blanchard's last acts before "going on leave" was to authorize the release of a news report that men from Roswell Air Base had recovered the wreckage of a flying disc.

(U.S. Air Force)

Carswell did not belong to any balloon. "He knew it was nothing made by us," she said, noting that "At first he thought it might be Russian because of the strange symbols on it. Later on, he realized it wasn't Russian either."

According to a Fort Worth Air Base document originally classified "Secret," one "Colonel Irvine, Assistant to the Chief of Staff, H.Q., Strategic Air Command (SAC)" visited General Ramey on July 10, 1947, on an undisclosed mission that almost certainly had something to do with the recovery of the crashed disc. Colonel Irvine (left) is shown here conferring with Colonel Blanchard at Roswell earlier in 1947.

(RAAF Yearbook, 1947, courtesy Walter Haut)

At the same time, Ramey's A-2 Division (Intelligence) chief, Colonel Alfred E. Kalberer, began making public appearances at meetings of several civic organizations around the Fort Worth area with a presentation designed to "counteract the growing hysteria towards flying discs."

On July 10, according to the records of the Fort Worth Army Air Base (which were originally classified as "Secret") "Colonel Irvine, Assistant to the Chief of Staff, H. Q., Strategic Air Command (SAC)" visited General Ramey on an undisclosed mission, which almost certainly included a discussion about the crashed disc.

Lieutenant Louis Bohanon, commanding Roswell's third photo laboratory unit, whose duties included the photographing of air crashes or damage to planes, left the base less than two weeks after the incident. It would appear that his group would have been called upon to make photographs of any unusual or unidentified crash in the area. But there is no record of any such photos. Lieutenant Bohanon was relieved of command by base special order No. 139 on July 18 and transferred to Hamilton Field, California.

Lieutenant Colonel Jennings, who temporarily assumed command of the base after Colonel Blanchard's departure, was to suffer a far stranger fate. Not too long after the Roswell Incident, while en route to England on a special assignment, his plane disappeared while flying over the Bermuda Triangle without sending a last message. No trace of the plane or of any survivors was ever found. Major Marcel had been scheduled to go on the same flight, but fortunately was pulled off upon the personal intervention of Colonel Blanchard.

The initial reports about the landing of a "flying disc" had already been widely spread by radio stations other than KSWS in Roswell, doubtlessly based on the first press release and in spite of the subsequent news blackout. Flight Major Hughie Green, of the British RAF, then en route by car from California to Philadelphia, was driving through New Mexico during July 1947. He remembers clearly what he heard on his car radio:

As I drove through New Mexico from west to east, I kept hearing these reports about a downed saucer on local stations as I came within the radius of each one. I was especially interested in the reports because of being in the RAF myself and remembering the wartime flap about "foo fighters"—the flying saucers of those days. The radio stations I was listening to were so on edge that they kept interrupting their regular broadcasts to give the latest developments. I am certain that one of the news broadcasts commented on the fact that the sheriff and his men were proceeding towards the field of the crash within sight of the wreckage.

I heard more reports as I entered the next state and there was further material, as I remember, in the press. But when I got to Philadelphia there was nothing at all about it in the papers or on the radio. I began asking reporter friends about it but they replied that they knew about it but heard that it had been hushed up.

As it was impossible to cover up the incident completely, a lively legend, if legend it is, has persisted to this day and it was to be expected that a book would be published about it as close as possible to the time of the incident. Such a book—*Behind the Flying Saucers* (Holt, 1950)—was written by Frank Scully, an author and syndicated columnist who based his information on the original

Flight Lieutenant (later Major) Hughie Green, RCAF, c. 1944. Green, a well-known British and Canadian radio personality and pilot, was driving through New Mexico at the time of the UFO crash and recalls hearing initial reports of its discovery on several local radio stations. He was amazed at how fast the story disappeared from the air after the first few reports.

(Hughie Green)

report of a saucer crash in New Mexico and the alleged recovery of the ship and the dead bodies of its alien crew by the U.S. military. It appears, perhaps because of his haste to finish the book while the subject was "hot," that Scully plunged into print without sufficient checking. As could be expected, his book, although financially eminently successful, was highly inaccurate and was soon "shot down" factually by the Air Force because of discrepancies in his research and incorrect information, including lack of names, mistakes concerning the area in which the incident occurred, and general unavailability of informants—something easier to overcome at the present time since the passing of the Freedom of Information Act along with a more liberal declassification policy. In his apparent haste to get into print, Scully placed the area of the crash near Aztec, in the upper western corner of the state, hundreds of miles from Roswell, and this mistake is still evident in UFO and other books published throughout the world.

Even so, Mrs. Frank Scully, widow of the writer, interviewed by Bill Moore at her home in June and December 1979, steadfastly maintained that the basic story behind her husband's book was correct and that he had been vilified because of it—particularly by J. P. Cahn, a "most unscrupulous journalist from San Francisco" who may have been paid off to do "the hatchet job" on Scully. It is true that Cahn's article on Scully and his book is full of exaggerations and inaccuracies. Unfortunately other journalists followed Cahn's account without bothering to check his accuracy. In any event, it was indeed Cahn's article that proved most damaging.

Cahn's condemnation of Scully's story, which first made print nearly two years after the appearance of the book itself, leans heavily upon the fact that at least two of Scully's informants were unscrupulous confidence men who were up to their ears in land fraud. This, added to the problems created by Roland Gelatt's blatant misquotation of several passages from Scully's book in a review by Gelatt which appeared in *Saturday Review* at the time the book was published, and a general condemnation of Scully's research methods by almost every one of the book's reviewers, seems to have been enough to convince other writers and journalists that the whole thing was a monstrous hoax and that Scully was its unfortunate victim. It is interesting to note, however, that virtually all of the book's detractors seem to have been content to rely on Gelatt's misquotations and Cahn's somewhat questionable assumption that land fraud was automatically proof of saucer fraud.

Although they readily condemned Scully for poor and sloppy research, none of them except Cahn seemed the least bit willing to do any of their own on the case; and Cahn's research was entirely limited to investigating the backgrounds of two of Scully's informants. In any event the damage was done and Scully's reputation suffered because of it.

There are indications however that Scully's book was taken somewhat more seriously in other circles—especially military. According to Mrs. Scully, a curious comment was made to her and her husband in late 1953 by Captain Edward Ruppelt, who at the time had just retired as head of Project Blue Book, the Air Force's third public attempt to deal with the flood of saucer sightings that continued to sweep the country after the initial flurry in 1947. "Confidentially," said Ruppelt, "of all the books that have been published about flying saucers, your book was the one that gave us the most headaches *because it was the closest to the truth.*" (Italics added)

Mrs. Scully said that her husband had received virtually all of his information from an unnamed government scientist whom Scully had befriended. She said that she had not heard from this individual for many years and did not even know whether he is still living, but she refused, even under promises of strict confidentiality, to reveal the name of this scientist. She did say, however, that this person had re-vealed to her and her husband about thirty years ago that one or more of the alien bodies from the crash had been transported to the Rosenwald Institute in Chicago for study.

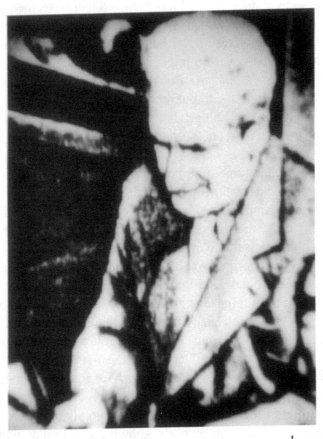

Author Frank Scully in 1950. It was Scully's well-meaning but poorly researched best seller *Behind the Flying Saucers* (1950) that brought to the attention of the American public the possibility that a flying saucer had crashed and that bodies and wreckage had been recovered by our government. His reputation was later to suffer because of what he wrote.

(Denver Post *Newsphoto)*

In short, Scully's book may be said to have provided the Air Force with an excellent opportunity to establish the entire legend as spurious or, at best, an erratic flight of imagination. It might also have served to stop other books at the source since *Behind the Flying Saucers* seemed to lack a firm foundation in investigation or fact. It might occur to an observer, nevertheless, that authorities concerned with the cover-up might even have encouraged the publication of *Behind the Flying Saucers* as a subterfuge aiding to discredit the initial reports. This is called "gray" propaganda in psychological warfare operations: although it appears to favor one's opponents its final effect is to discredit or confuse them.

At about this same time Fletcher Pratt, author and leading military historian, initiated additional rumor waves in the press by announcing, in the early part of 1950, that he had obtained "through confidential channels" information that a flying saucer had crashed to earth and that bodies of a vaguely human appearance and about thirty-five inches tall had been found dead in the wreckage.

This further reference to a Roswell-type incident was, of course, denied in official circles with the customary vehemence. However, it must not be forgotten that Fletcher Pratt was a reputable military historian with a historian's regard for the highest possible accuracy of information and therefore would have been reticent to accept a report dealing with startling information from an unreliable source. Pratt was also (to the author's knowledge) familiar with the requirements of military security and, even if at first convinced of the accuracy of his source, could have been later persuaded to let the matter drop in the interests of security.

In any event, the commotion engendered by the alleged capture of a UFO appears to have resulted in a continued close Army Air Force surveillance of UFOs with reports running into the thousands, all of which finally culminated in the so-called Condon Report of 1969 (an Air Force project contracted to the University of Colorado), which finally determined, according to their press release, that only 10 percent of the UFO sightings investigated by them seemed to resist all logical explanation. (A more rigorous examination of the report itself, however, would seem to suggest that the actual number of sightings lacking reasonable explanation was somewhat closer to 30 percent.) In any case, it was determined (using the Condon Report as an excuse) that the effort and expense of Air Force investigation did not seem to justify the continued existence of an Air Force project (in this case, Project Blue Book) designed to publicly investigate UFOs. Partly as a result of Condon's recommendations (which in fact appear to have been somewhat rigged beforehand by the Air Force) Blue Book was canceled on December 17, 1969, and the Air Force, after some twenty-two years, ceased to have any *visible* interest in the UFO phenomenon.

One particularly interesting aspect of the Air Force's investigation of UFOs during the Blue Book years was Air Force regulation 200-2, instituted in August 1953 and containing detailed information to Air Force personnel on how to cope with UFOs, including pages of checklists and diagrams enabling the witness to furnish a description. Among these instructions concerning sightings of UFOs (which officially don't exist, but here's what to do when you encounter one) some especially pertinent directives, addressed to base commanders, are included concerning the release of UFO information to the general public. AFR 200-2, paragraph nine:

In response to local inquiries, it is permissible to

inform news media representatives on UFOBs [i.e., UFOs] when the object is positively identified as a familiar object. . . . For those objects which are not explainable, only the fact that ATIC [Air Technical Intelligence Command] will analyze the data is worthy of release, due to the many unknowns involved. . . .

One might reflect that if Major Marcel, Lieutenant Haut, and Roswell Base Commander Colonel Blanchard had had the advantage of having AFR 200-2 to consult and guide them, no public uproar regarding the Roswell Incident— the echoes of which can still be discerned—would have taken place.

Since 1947, UFOs have been seen by the thousands every year throughout the world and have been blamed for or suspected of causing the disappearance of ships and planes in the Bermuda Triangle, of the capture and brain-washing of human beings, interference with communications and electric systems, and of being participants in ray-gun versus machine-gun and rocket fights in a number of countries. (The earthlings lost.) It is therefore especially notable to remember that one of the first modern reports, the reputed UFO crash in New Mexico, was the most unusual visitation of all and took place within one hundred miles of an air force base.

In any case, since the UFO security procedures had not been sufficiently established in 1947, the incident was widely disseminated before it was smothered. Like many other legends, it seems to possess an extraordinary power of survival and has been repeatedly revived, sometimes, as we shall see, by direct presidential request. Furthermore, witnesses of the incident and secondary witnesses—those who first spoke to the direct witnesses—are still alive and remember details with commendable recall. A cross-check of their recollections indicates a general agreement with the different aspects contained in the first reports of the fallen disc, or whatever it really was.

4

Witnesses Speak—
the Town Remembers

Barney Barnett, a resident of Socorro, New Mexico, a civil engineer working for the federal government in soil conservation, was one of the first witnesses to arrive at the site of the fallen saucer, sometime in the morning of July 3, 1947.

While living in New Mexico, Barney and his wife, Ruth, had become close friends with L. W. "Vern" Maltais and his wife, Jean Swedmark Maltais. Vern was "on assignment with the military" in New Mexico at this time.

In February 1950, during a visit by the Maltaises to Socorro, Barnett told his friends an extraordinary story. Before telling them, however, he cautioned them not to repeat it. Barnett claimed to have personally witnessed a flying-saucer crash in the Socorro area—that he had seen it and seen dead bodies that were not human beings. Then the area was quickly sealed off and the bodies and wreckage removed by the military.

Although three decades have passed since Barnett told his strange tale to the Maltaises, they remember it very well, especially as it was underscored by the many UFO sightings reported in New Mexico at the time. Both the Maltaises spoke highly of Barnett's character. He was older than they were, very conservative, and quite sure of himself—definitely not the type to go about spreading wild rumors. But, the Maltaises recalled, Barnett definitely said he had seen the thing on the ground. According to the Maltaises, this is what Barnett told them:

I was out on assignment, working near Magdalena, New Mexico, one morning when light reflecting off some sort of large metallic object caught my eye. Thinking that a plane may have crashed during the night, I went over to where it was—about a mile, perhaps a mile and a quarter away on flat desert land. By the time I got there, I realized it wasn't a plane at all, but some sort of metallic, disc-shaped object about twenty-five or thirty feet across. While I was looking at it and trying to decide what it was, some other people came up from the other direction and began looking around it too. They told me later that they were a part of an archaeological research team from some eastern university [the University of Pennsylvania] and that they too had first thought a plane had crashed. They were all over the place look-ing at the wreck.

I noticed that they were standing around looking at some dead bodies that had fallen to the ground. I think there were others [dead bodies] in the machine, which was a kind of metallic instrument of some sort—a kind of disc. It was not all that big. It seemed to be made of a metal that looked like dirty stainless steel. The machine had been split open by explosion or impact.

I tried to get close to see what the bodies were like. They were all dead as far as I could see and there were bodies inside and outside the vehicle. The ones outside had been tossed out by the impact. They were like humans but they were not humans. The heads were round, the eyes were small, and they had no hair. The eyes were oddly spaced. They were quite small by our standards and their heads were larger in proportion to their bodies than ours. Their clothing seemed to be one-piece and gray in color. You couldn't see any zippers, belts, or buttons. They seemed to me to be all males and there were a number of them. I was close enough to touch them but I didn't—I was escorted away before I could look at them anymore.

While we were looking at them a military officer drove up in a truck with a driver and took control. He told everybody that the Army was taking over and to get out of the way. Other military personnel came up and cordoned off the area. We were told to leave the area and not to talk to anyone whatever about what we had seen . . . that it was our patriotic duty to remain silent. . . .

Mrs. Maltais interrupted at this point to add:

Barnett said that he was out in the field when he saw this thing, and that there were other individuals there with him. I think he said that the individuals he talked to there were from the University of Pennsylvania. They were doing some digs in the New Mexico area and were involved with this thing only because they were in the area when it crashed.

World War I Army ID of Grady L. "Barney" Barnett, who broke a pledge of secrecy to tell friends he had witnessed the crash of an unidentified flying object in New Mexico in 1947.

(Mrs. Alice Knight)

Grady L. "Barney" Barnett in front of his Socorro, New Mexico, house in 1945, barely two years before he would be a witness to one of the most startling events of man's history.

(Mrs. Alice Knight)

Grave site of Barney and his wife, Ruth Barnett, in Dalhart, Texas.
(W. L. Moore)

The object was a metallic-like instrument of some sort. The individuals were quite small by our standards. Their heads were larger in proportion to their bodies compared to our human standards. I remember vividly that Barnett had been told to say absolutely nothing and he had not done so for several years until he shared his experience with us in 1950. We were very close friends, perhaps the closest he had.

Barnett called the creatures "males." There was no mention of females. There were a number of them, but I can't remember how many he said there were. He repeated several times that their eyes were small and oddly spaced.

The object was soon moved away from the crash site. They brought in a large truck. Whoever was involved with it asked the spectators to leave. This included the University of Pennsylvania people. Everyone was told to leave the area and not to talk about it to anyone, because to do so would be unpatriotic.

View of the Plains of San Agustin, near Socorro, New Mexico—crash site of the "Barnett device" in 1947, and currently the location of the National Radio Astronomy Observatory's Very Large Array (VLA) radio telescope program for listening in on the universe. According to the NRAO, the site's location was specifically chosen because of the "extremely low level of manmade electrical interference" in the area.

(W. L. Moore)

When asked if she recalled in what part of New Mexico Barnett had said the crash had occurred, Mrs. Maltais answered: "No, I don't exactly recall. It was somewhere out of Socorro. He may have said exactly, but I don't recall. I remember he said it was prairie—'the Flats' is the way he put it. Definitely not in a mountainous area. Barnett traveled all over New Mexico, but did most of his work in the area directly west of Socorro."

As Barney Barnett's reported version of the incident is so complete and ties in so neatly with other reports it is pertinent to consider his reputation in the area and whether

or not he was especially imaginative or visionary.

Grady Landon (Barney) Barnett worked as an engineer in the area for the U.S. Soil Conservation Service for twenty years until his retirement in 1957. He was a veteran of World War I (Second Lieutenant, 313 Engineers, AEF) and past commander of the American Legion Post at Mosquero, New Mexico—certainly a model of a conservative respected citizen.

Holm Bursum, Jr., bank executive, former mayor of Socorro, and son of Holm Bursum, Sr., former U.S. senator from New Mexico, was not unaware of the atomic or space age, as his cattle were exposed to fallout from the first 1945 A-bomb test at Alamogordo, which caused them to turn spotted white and subsequently to be shipped to Oak Ridge National Laboratory for study. When interviewed by Moore in 1979, he immediately recalled having known Barnett quite well, and spoke highly of him. Asked

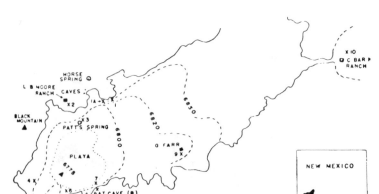

Map of the San Agustin Plains area near Socorro, New Mexico, showing the location of archaeological sites excavated by the 1946–48 expedition.

(American Antiquity Magazine)

about the possibility that Barnett's crashed UFO account may have been true, Bursum replied: "A tale like that would have been fantastic all right but I would have to say that anything he said would have to be true to the best of his knowledge."

Lee Garner, former cowboy and later sheriff of Socorro County, remembers Barney Barnett favorably and especially remembers the archaeological expedition, doubtlessly because of his own interest in Indian archaeology. He thought the expedition was from Michigan, but said there may have been Pennsylvania students involved with it. John Greenwald, a former federal government employee and now a retired farmer in Socorro County, recalled that Barnett worked primarily in a map area to the west of Socorro called the Plains of San Agustin, also called locally "the Flats," and believed that the incident had taken place there.

J. F. "Fleck" Danley of Magdalena, New Mexico, was more specific:

Barnett was an engineer and worked under me out of Magdalena in the 1940s and early fifties. He was a good man . . . one of the most honest men I ever knew.

QUESTION (by Moore): *Did Barnett ever say anything about a flying saucer?*

Yes, there was one time. Barney came into the office one afternoon all kind of excited and said to me: "You know those flying-saucer things they've been talking about, Fleck . . .? Well, they're real." Then he said something about he's just had a look at one of them. I was real busy at the time and wasn't in any mood to buy a story like that, so I just turned around to him and said: "Bull - - - -!" and went back to work. All he told me was that he saw it. I wasn't prepared to believe it at the time and after I had said "Bull - - - -" he didn't explain anything else about it. I got to thinking about it later that maybe I shouldn't have been so rough with him because he wasn't the sort to go around making up stories like that, but when I asked him about it a day or so later all he said was out on the flats, that it looked like a saucer, and that he didn't care to talk any more about it.

Fleck felt he could remember the date of the incident if given time to think about it. In a subsequent interview conducted in his living room some four months later, he chuckled and said: "Yes, I recall it now. It had to have been sometime in the early summer of 1947. I didn't believe any of it when Barney first told me, but we did talk about it some later on, even though I know I told you before that we hadn't. I'd have to say from what he told me that I believe it now. I never knew Barney to lie . . . not about anything." When asked if he could repeat what Barney had told him, Danley replied: "I'll have to think on that awhile. Maybe I've told you enough already."

Perhaps some of the most important testimony in the matter of the crashed disc comes from Major (now Lieutenant Colonel) Jesse A. Marcel, ranking staff officer in charge of intelligence at the Roswell Army Air Base at the time of the incident. Marcel, now retired and living in Houma, Louisiana, had been flying since 1928 and, in his own words, was "familiar with virtually everything that flew." As one of the few cartographers familiar with both the making and interpreting of aerial maps before World War II, he was sent to intelligence school by the Army Air Force following Pearl Harbor and proved to be so capable a student that, upon completion of training, he was retained as an instructor. Fifteen months later, he applied for and was granted combat duty, and went to New Guinea, where he became intelligence officer for his bomber squadron and later for his entire group. Flying as bombardier, waist gunner, and pilot, he logged 468 hours of combat flying in B-24s, was awarded five air medals for shooting down five enemy aircraft, and was himself shot down once (on his third mission).

Toward the end of the war, Marcel was chosen to become a part of the 509th Bomb Wing of the U.S. Army Air Force, the world's only atomic bomb group at the time, and one of the few "élite" groups in the U.S. military, where all officers and enlisted men were literally hand-picked for their jobs and required high-security clearances. As a part of this group in 1946, he was instrumental in handling security for the 1946 Kwajalein atom-bomb tests (Operation Crossroads) and was awarded a commendation by the U.S. Navy for his work.

In recent interviews (Moore and Stanton Friedman, February, May, and December 1979) he remembered some interesting details concerning his own connection with the Roswell Incident and the intriguing possibility that either there was a second disc that exploded in the air or that material fell, after an explosion, from the disc described in Barnett's account before that object apparently crashed to the earth some distance to the west.

QUESTION: *Major Marcel, did you personally see a crashed UFO?*

I saw a lot of wreckage but no complete machine. Whatever it was had to have exploded in the air above ground level. It had disintegrated before it hit the ground. The wreckage was scattered over an area of about three quarters of a mile long and several hundred feet wide.

How did the Roswell Base know about the crash at Brazel's ranch?

We heard about it on July 7 when we got a call from the county sheriff's office at Roswell. I was eating lunch at the officers' club when the call came through saying that I should go out and talk to Brazel. The sheriff said that Brazel had told him that something had exploded over Brazel's ranch and that there was a lot of debris scattered around.

I finished my lunch and went into town to talk to this fellow. When I had heard what he had to say, I decided that this was a matter that had better be brought to the attention of the colonel [Colonel Blanchard] right away and let him decide what ought to be done. I wanted Brazel

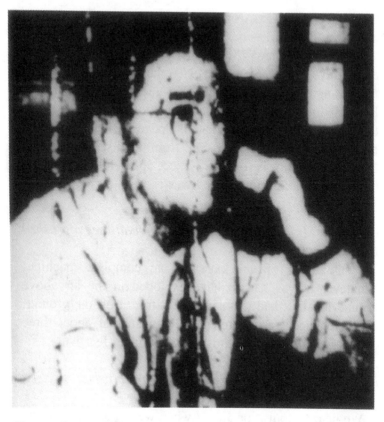

Chaves County (New Mexico) Sheriff George Wilcox of Roswell, shown here on July 8, 1947. Wilcox's office received calls from "all around the world" following a Roswell AAF Base announcement that the wreckage of a crashed flying disc had been recovered on a nearby ranch.

(Roswell Daily Record *Newsphoto)*

to accompany me back to the base with his truck, but he said he had some things to do first and could he meet me somewhere in an hour or so. I arranged for him to meet me at the sheriff's office, and went back to see the colonel.

In my discussion with the colonel, we determined that a

downed aircraft of some unusual sort might be involved, so the colonel said I had better get out there, and to take whatever I needed and go. I and a CIC [Counter-Intelligence Corps] agent from West Texas by the name of Cavitt [Marcel couldn't recall his first name] followed this man out to his ranch, with me driving my staff car [a '42 Buick] and Cavitt in a Jeep Carry-all. There were almost no roads, and at spots we literally had to go right across country. It was as close to the middle of nowhere as you could get. Anyhow, we got there very late in the afternoon and had to spend the night with this fellow. All we had to eat was some cold pork and beans and some crackers.

Brazel lived on the southeast side of Corona—quite far. The closest town was thirty miles away. He lived in a dinky house on a sheep ranch—no radio, no telephone—lived there by himself most of the time. His wife and kids lived in Tularosa or Carrizozo [Note: It was Tularosa.] so the children would have some place to attend school.

It seems to me that Brazel told me that he thought he had heard an odd explosion late in the evening several days earlier during an electrical storm, but paid no special attention to it at the time because he had attributed it to just a freak part of the storm. He didn't find the wreckage until the next morning.

On Saturday, July 5, 1947, Brazel went into town—Corona. While he was there he heard stories about flying saucers having been seen all over the area. He began to think that's what had come down on his ranch, but I don't know whether he said anything about it to anyone at the time.

On Sunday, July 6, Brazel decided he had better go into town and report this to someone. When he got there, he went to the Chaves County sheriff's office and told the story to the sheriff. It was the sheriff, George Wilcox, who called me at the base. I was eating lunch at the time and had just sat down when the phone rang.

Do you think that what you saw was a weather balloon?

It was not. I was pretty well acquainted with most everything that was in the air at that time, both ours and foreign. I was also acquainted with virtually every type of weather-observation or radar tracking device being used by either the civilians or the military. It was definitely not a weather or tracking device, nor was it any sort of plane or missile. What it was we didn't know. We just picked up the fragments. It was something I had never seen before, or since, for that matter. I didn't know what it was, but it certainly wasn't anything built by us and it most certainly wasn't any weather balloon.

Can you describe the materials that you found on the site?

There was all kinds of stuff—small beams about three eighths or a half inch square with some sort of hieroglyphics on them that nobody could decipher. These looked something like balsa wood, and were of about the same weight, except that they were not wood at all. They were very hard, although flexible, and would not burn. There was a great deal of an unusual parchment-like substance which was brown in color and extremely strong, and a great number of small pieces of a metal like tinfoil, except that it wasn't tinfoil. I was interested in electronics and kept looking for something that resembled instruments or electronic equipment, but I didn't find anything. One of the other fellows, Cavitt, I think, found a black, metallic-looking box several inches square. As there was no apparent way to open this, and since it didn't appear to be an instrument package of any sort (it too was very light-weight), we threw it in with the rest of the stuff. I don't know what eventually happened to the box, but it went along with the rest of the material we eventually took to Fort Worth.

What was especially interesting about the material?

One thing that impressed me about the debris was the fact that a lot of it looked like parchment. It had little numbers with symbols that we had to call hieroglyphics because I could not understand them. They could not be read, they were just like symbols, something that meant something, and they were not all the same, but the same general pattern, I would say. They were pink and purple. They looked like they were.painted on. These little numbers could not be broken, could not be burned. I even took my cigarette lighter and tried to burn the material we found that resembled parchment and balsa, but it would not burn—wouldn't even smoke. But something that is even more astounding is that the pieces of metal that we brought back were so thin, just like the tinfoil in a pack of cigarettes. I didn't pay too much attention to that at first, until one of the boys came to me and said: "You know that metal that was in there? I tried to bend the stuff and it won't bend. I even tried it with a sledgehammer. You can't make a dent on it." . . . This particular piece of metal was about two feet long and maybe a foot wide. It was so light it weighed practically nothing, that was true of all the material that was brought up, it weighed practically nothing . . . it was so thin. So I tried to bend the stuff. We did all we could to bend it. It would not bend and you could not tear it or cut it either. We even tried making a dent in it with a sixteen-pound sledgehammer, and there was still no dent in it. . . . It's still a mystery to me what the whole thing was. Now by bend, I mean crease. It was possible to flex this stuff back and forth, even to wrinkle it, but you could not put a crease in it that would stay, nor could you dent it at all. I would almost have to describe it as a metal with plastic properties. One of the fellows tried to put some of the pieces together— like a jigsaw puzzle. He managed to get about ten square feet together, but it wasn't enough to get any idea of the general shape of the object itself. Whatever it was, it was big.

What did you do with the material you had picked up?

We collected all the debris we could handle. When we had filled the Carry-all, I began to fill the trunk and back seat of the Buick. That afternoon [July 7] we headed back to Roswell and arrived there in the early evening.

When we arrived there, we discovered that the story that we had found a flying disc had leaked out ahead of us. We had an eager-beaver PIO [public information officer] on the base who had taken it upon himself to call the AP on this thing. We had several calls that night, and one reporter even came to the house, but of course I couldn't confirm anything to them over the phone, and the man who came to the house my wife sent over to see the colonel. The next morning that written press release went out, and after that things really hit the fan. The phone rang right off the hook. I heard that the brass fried him later on for putting out that press release, but then I can't say so for sure. . . .

Anyway, that next afternoon we loaded everything into a B-29 on orders from Colonel Blanchard and flew it all to Fort Worth. I was scheduled to fly it all the way to Wright

Field in Ohio, but when we got to Carswell at Fort Worth, the general nixed it. He took control at this point, told the press it was all a weather balloon, and ordered me not to talk to the press under any circumstances. I was pulled off the flight and someone else was assigned to fly the stuff up to Wright [Patterson] Field. Everything was sent to Wright-Patterson for analysis.

Just after we got to Carswell, Fort Worth, we were told to bring some of this stuff up to the general's office—that he wanted to take a look at it. We did this and spread it out on the floor on some brown paper.

What we had was only a very small portion of the debris—there was a whole lot more. There was half a B-29-ful outside. General Ramey allowed some members of the press in to take a picture of this stuff. They took one picture of me on the floor holding up some of the less-interesting metallic debris. The press was allowed to photograph this, but were not allowed far enough into the room to touch it. The stuff in that one photo was pieces of the actual stuff we had found. It was not a staged photo. Later, they cleared out our wreckage and substituted some of their own. Then they allowed more photos. Those photos were taken while the actual wreckage was already on its way to Wright Field. I was not in these. I believe these were taken with the general and one of his aides. I've seen a lot of weather balloons, but I've never seen one like that before. And I don't think they ever did either.

Let's go back to how the press and radio people got involved. Can we go over that again?

It was the public information officer, Haut I believe his name was, who called the AP and later wrote the press release. I heard he wasn't authorized to do this, and I believe he was severely reprimanded for it, I think all the way from Washington. We had calls from everywhere—all over the world. It was General Ramey who put up the cover story about the balloon just to get the press off our backs. The press was told it was just a balloon and that the flight to Wright-Patterson was canceled; but all that really happened was that I was removed from the flight and someone else took it up to W-P. I wasn't even allowed to talk to the press except to say what the general had told me to say. They all wanted to ask me questions, and I couldn't tell them anything.

So what you're saying is that this whole weather-balloon thing was nothing but a cover-up?

Well, one thing that I want to point out is that the newsmen saw very little of the material—and none of the important things that had hieroglyphics, or markings, on them. They didn't see that because it wasn't there. They wanted me to tell them about it but I couldn't say anything. When the general came in he told me not to say anything, that he would handle it. He told the newsmen: "Yes, that's the weather balloon." So the newsmen had to take his word for it because they had nothing else to go by. They tried to get me to talk about it, but the general had told me not to say anything and I couldn't say anything. That's when the general told me: "It's best you go back to Roswell. You have duties to perform there. We'll handle it from here. . . ."*

---

*After duly noting the general's strong hint, Major Marcel returned to Roswell immediately and maintained a commendable silence for years thereafter.

In October 1947, just three months after the Roswell Incident, Marcel was suddenly transferred to Washington, D.C., over Colonel Blanchard's objections. Once there, he was quickly promoted to lieutenant colonel (in December) and assigned to a Special Weapons Program that was busy collecting air samples from throughout the world and analyzing them in an effort to detect whether the Russians had exploded their first nuclear bomb. "When we finally detected that there had been an atomic explosion, it was my job to write the report on it," related Marcel. "In fact, when President Truman went on the air to declare that the Russians had exploded a nuclear device, it was my report that he was reading from."

Upon being asked whether he knew if the Brazel-ranch wreckage was connected with the report that a saucer had crashed near Socorro at about the same time, Marcel answered:

I heard about that but I could not verify such an occurrence from my own experience. Of course, if another military group had become involved with a larger piece of wreckage, there would be no reason for me to be informed about it officially. All I can verify is what I saw and, I repeat, the material I saw came from no weather balloon.

Would anyone else remember anything about what you found on the Brazel ranch?

My son may remember something. He was about twelve then and he saw some of the stuff we took from the site before it was packed off.

Major (later Lieutenant Colonel) Jesse A. Marcel, S-2 (Intelligence) officer, Roswell Army Air Base, 1947. Major Marcel was in charge of a July 1947 investigative expedition that recovered the first pieces of wreckage from what appears to have been a UFO crash.

(RAAF Yearbook, 1947, courtesy Walter Haut)

Major Marcel's son is now a doctor in Helena, Montana. As a young boy Dr. Marcel was naturally interested in flying and also in space travel. He was fascinated by what his father had brought home and the reports that a vehicle and wreckage from space had come down near the Roswell Base, but he did not have much opportunity to examine it. Dr. Marcel remembers:

Dad got a call to go out and investigate a downed aircraft or something like that. He was gone a couple of days and returned with a van and part of a car filled with wreckage and debris.

The material was foil-like stuff, very thin, metallic-like but not metal, and very tough. There was also some structural-like material too—beams and so on. Also a quantity of black plastic material which looked organic in nature.

Dad returned toward evening. He was gone all one night and most of the next day. He had a 1942 Buick and a Carry-all trailer, and both were loaded with this material which was only a small fraction of the total material.

Dr. Marcel recalled that he was about eleven at this time. When asked if he had managed to save a piece of this material, he replied:

You know, I could have kicked myself a thousand times over for not doing so. Dad said it was classified stuff and not to take any, so I didn't. But I sure wish I had.

Did Dr. Marcel recall hearing anything more about the incident after that?

Yes. The story leaked out and we were bombarded with reporters, etc. I wasn't too involved in this. My main impression was that the metal objects and strips were from some kind of machine not a weather balloon. I was told that it was some type of aircraft, but it wasn't any type we were familiar with—that's for sure. Dad said that the speed of impact was not in keeping with any type of aircraft we had at that time.

Several weeks later, in April 1979, Dr. Marcel remembered something else:

In reference to the UFO incident of 1947 or 1948 I omitted one startling description of the wreckage for fear it might have been the fanciful imagination of a twelve-year-old. Imprinted along the edge of some of the beam remnants there were hieroglyphic-type characters. I recently questioned my father about this, and he recalled seeing these characters also, and even described them as being a pink or purplish-pink color. Egyptian hieroglyphics would be a close visual description of the characters seen, except I don't think there were any animal figures present as there are in true Egyptian hieroglyphics.

I keep wondering if some remnants of the crash might still be lying on the New Mexico desert floor. According to my father, some of it was left behind when he and his crew investigated the air-crash site. I suspect, however, that after the true nature of the craft became known to Air Force Intelligence, the whole site was gone over with a vacuum cleaner.

As you know, my dad brought a portion of the wreckage into the house and spread it over the kitchen floor, trying to piece some of the larger fragments together. There were quite literally piles of metallic scrap along with bits of a black, brittle residue that looked like plastic that had either melted or burned. The task was hopeless because there was far too much debris for one kitchen floor to hold.

I doubt if all the smaller fragments were picked up from the kitchen, and, indeed, my mother remarked that some of it was probably swept out the back door. About that time we poured a concrete slab around the back door for a patio. I don't recall whether this was before or after the incident, but if it was shortly after, what better way to preserve some of these fragments that were swept away? [Chances of] recovery of anything would be vanishingly small, but not zero. . . .

Although this would not be the first time in the chronicles of archaeology that potentially and incalculably valuable shards or records had been unconsciously destroyed, researchers would no doubt meet with some difficulties explaining to the present owners of the then Marcel house the imperative need for breaking up the patio piece by piece in order to locate writings from space.

Walter Haut, now the proprietor of the W. H. Art Gallery in Roswell, although the base PIO at the time of the incident, was not a witness. His activities were mainly limited to the uproar occasioned by the arrival of the apparently interplanetary visitors. In interviews during March and June 1979, his recollections ran as follows:

Lieutenant Haut was called by Colonel William Blanchard and directed to write and distribute a news release to the effect that the AAF had recovered the remains of a crashed flying disc. When he asked whether he could see the object in question he was told by Colonel Blanchard that his request was impossible. He wrote the story and distributed the release.

Haut was informed that Major Marcel had been on the plane that had taken the recovered material to Fort Worth, but Haut did not go. He was ordered to stay behind and "answer the telephone" (one remembers that he was only a lieutenant) which he did continuously for the next eight hours, receiving calls for information from all over the world, including one, he remembers, from Hong Kong. When Colonel Blanchard learned of this now international news explosion he "hit the ceiling" and told Lieutenant Haut: "If there is any way you can get them to shut up on it, then go ahead and do it." The pressure ceased when the "weather balloon" story was issued from Fort Worth accompanied by General Ramey's definitive denials to the press and over Radio WBAP from Fort Worth.

Haut resigned his commission in April 1948 on learning that he was about to be transferred. (N.B. He was promoted to captain before he left the service. However, he was not promoted before he signified his willingness to resign.) A Sergeant Edward Gregory, who worked in the Public Information Office with Lieutenant Haut at the time of the incident, observed in a phone interview with Stan Friedman from his home at Livermore, California, that he never quite understood why Lieutenant Haut had left the service and that if he had stayed in the Air Force he would really have made it because he was exceptionally sharp. Colonel Blanchard, Sergeant Gregory said, was "top-notch . . . first-rate, and wouldn't have suggested any press release unless he was damn sure he wasn't dealing with any weather balloon."

The series of denials of the first release might be considered a fairly normal mistake and be excused on the grounds of a nationwide UFO "flap" at the time, however far this would have taken the local command from the army tradition of "no excuses—no explanations." But there were to be a variety of other direct and indirect witnesses, and means would have to have been found, if the upper echelons had decided to wipe out the story, to silence effectively the other witnesses, either through ridicule or having them change their stories.

One person who should certainly have had firsthand information about the alleged craft would be William W. "Mac" Brazel, the rancher who discovered the strange pieces of wreckage on his land, and the person ultimately responsible for bringing the entire matter to the attention of Major Marcel at Roswell. Although the elder Brazel died in 1963, his son and daughter-in-law, Bill and Shirley Brazel of Capitan, New Mexico, recall the incident well. Bill Brazel is an employee of Texas Instruments and spends the better part of his time working away from home as a geoseismologist in Alaska's North Slope oil region.

Moore: (Interviews conducted in March, June, and
December of 1979.)

QUESTION: *Mr. Brazel, what can you tell me about
your father's experience in discovering the wreckage of
some sort of aerial device out on the ranch?*

Well, actually I can't tell you the whole story about that
because I don't know all of it. Father was very reluctant to
talk about it at all, and what I know is only what I could
manage to get out of him over the years before he died. He
took the most part of what he knew to the grave with him.
They [the military] swore him to secrecy, you know, and
he took that very seriously. A good indication of just how
seriously is that he would never even talk to Mother about
it. To tell the truth, Shirley here was the closest to him of
any of the family and if he was going to tell anyone at all
about what he knew, it would have been her. But he never
told her the whole story either, so unless the military
chooses to come out in the open with what they know,
we're likely never to find out any more about it.

Actually, we first learned about it when we picked up a
copy of the Albuquerque *Journal* one evening and saw
Dad's picture on the front page. There was another story
about it in the Lincoln County *News*. Shirley said: "My
God, what's he got himself into now?" and I said: "I
don't know, but maybe we had better go over to the ranch
tomorrow and find out." We had just been married at the
time and were living in Albuquerque. Anyhow, when we
got there Dad wasn't there. There was nobody there. Well,
we knew he was in Roswell from what the paper had said,
so I decided I had better stay and look after the ranch till
he got home again. Shirley went on back to Albuquerque
that evening. By Monday [July 14] when Dad still hadn't
returned, I began to get concerned, and that was when I

went over to Corona and made a few phone calls to find out what was going on. I was told not to worry, that Dad was O.K. and that he ought to be coming back to the ranch in the next day or so.

July 1947 photo of rancher W. W. "Mac" Brazel who first discovered the crash debris while checking fences on his ranch.

(Mrs. Lorraine Brazel Ferguson)

Sure enough, he did, but when he got there, he wouldn't say hardly anything about where he had been or what he had done there. He seemed very disgusted about it all, and was in no mood to talk about it. "You saw that paper," he said. "What you read there is all you need to know. That way, nobody will bother you about it." Later on, he said that he had "found this thing and turned it in to Roswell" and they shut him up for about a week because of it. I can still hear him: "Gosh," he said, "I just tried to do a good deed and they put me in jail for it." Then he said that if we had read it in the papers, then we knew all there was to tell. He said they had told him to shut up because it was important to our country and was the patriotic thing to do, and so that's what he intended to do. He did say that they had shut him up in a room and wouldn't let him out. He was very discouraged and upset about the way they had treated him. They even gave him a complete "head-to-foot army physical" before they would let him come home.

What I finally got out of him came in bits and pieces over the years, and from what I can piece together, what happened was this:

Dad was in the ranch house with two of the younger kids late one evening when a terrible lightning storm came up. He said it was the worst lightning storm he had ever seen [and you can be sure he had seen a lot of them], not much rain with it, just lightning—strike after strike. He said it seemed strange that the lightning kept wanting to strike the same spots time and again, almost as if there was something attracting it to those spots—he thought maybe underground mineral deposits or something. Anyway, in the middle of this storm there was an odd sort of explosion, not like the ordinary thunder, but different. He said he didn't think too much about it at the time because the storm was so bad that he just guessed it was some freak lightning strike, but later he wondered about it. Anyhow, the next morning while riding out over the pasture to check on some sheep, he came across this collection of wreckage scattered over a patch of land about a quarter mile long or so, and several hundred feet wide. He said to me once that it looked like that whatever this stuff had come from had blown up. He also said that from the way this wreckage was scattered, you could tell it was traveling "an airline route to Socorro," which is off to the southwest of the ranch.

At first he didn't recognize the importance of it, and it was only after a day or so of thinking on it that he decided he had better go back and have a closer look.

It was then that he picked some of it up and brought it back to the ranch house. That evening he went over and talked to Proctor [Floyd Proctor, Brazel's nearest neighbor] about it. But Proctor wasn't interested in coming over to look at it, and Dad was more curious than ever. The next night he went into Corona, and it was then, during a discussion with my uncle, Hollis Wilson, and someone that he knew from Alamogordo, that he first heard about the flying-saucer reports that were sweeping this area at that time. Both Hollis and this other fellow from Alamogordo thought that there was a chance that Dad had picked up the pieces of one of these things, and they advised him to go to the authorities with it. Dad was still not convinced, but he knew this stuff was like nothing he had ever seen before, so the next day he rounded up the two kids and took off for Roswell by way of Tularosa, where he stopped off and left the kids with Mother. I believe his original intention was to go to Roswell and buy a new Jeep pickup truck—he certainly wouldn't have made the trip just on account of the stuff he had found—but I don't believe he bargained for what he got himself into. One thing's for sure, he didn't get the pickup on that trip anyhow.

Now some of the news reports have it that he went to Roswell to sell wool. I don't know where they got that story, or some of the other information they printed along with it, but I can say for sure that Dad never sold any wool in Roswell. He always contracted for all his wool with some company up in Utah, and they always picked up the wool at the ranch with their own trucks. Anyway, I know he didn't go there to sell wool—it was about trading his pickup that he went.

Did he ever describe what he had found to you?

No, not exactly; but then, he didn't need to since I had some of it myself. He had showed me the place where this stuff had come down, but of course you couldn't see anything there since the Air Force had had a whole platoon of men out there picking up every piece and shred that they could find. Still, every time I rode through that particular pasture I would make a point to look. Seems like every time after a good rain I would manage to find a piece or two that they had overlooked. After about a year and a half or two years I had managed to accumulate quite a small collection—about enough that if you were to lay it out on this tabletop it would take up about as much area as your briefcase there.

Can you describe what you found?

Yes, I can. There were several different types of stuff. Of course all I had was small bits and pieces, but one thing that I can say about it was that it sure was light in weight. It weighed almost nothing. There was some wooden-like particles I picked up. These were like balsa wood in weight, but a bit darker in color and much harder. You know the thing about wood is that the harder it gets, the heavier it is. Mahogany, for example, is quite heavy. This stuff, on the other hand, weighed nothing, yet you couldn't scratch it with your fingernail like ordinary balsa, and you couldn't break it either. It was pliable, but wouldn't break. Of course, all I had was a few splinters. It never occurred to me to try to burn it so I don't know if it would burn or not.

There were also several bits of a metal-like substance, something on the order of tinfoil except that this stuff wouldn't tear and was actually a bit darker in color than tinfoil—more like lead foil, except very thin and extremely lightweight. The odd thing about this foil was that you could wrinkle it and lay it back down and it immediately resumed its original shape. It was quite pliable, yet you couldn't crease or bend it like ordinary metal. It was almost more like a plastic of some sort, except that it was definitely metallic in nature. I don't know what it was, but I do know that Dad once said the Army had told him that they had definitely established it was not anything made by us.

Then there was some thread-like material. It looked like silk and there were several pieces of it. It was not large enough to call it string, but yet not so small as sewing thread either. To all appearances it was silk, except that it wasn't silk. Whatever it was, it too was a very strong material. You could take it in two hands and try to snap it, but it wouldn't snap at all. Nor did it have strands or fibers like silk thread would have. This was more like a wire— all one piece or substance. In fact, I suppose it could have been a sort of wire—that thought never occurred to me before.

This stuff was something I had never seen the like of before. None of this stuff had an exactly natural appearance about it, it was more like something synthetic now that I think about it.

Was there any writing or markings on any of the material you had?

No, not on what I had. But Dad did say one time that there were what he called "figures" on some of the pieces he found. He often referred to the petroglyphs the ancient Indians drew on rocks around here as "figures" too, and I think that's what he meant to compare them with.

What ever became of this collection of yours? Do you still have it?

Now that's the curious part of the story. No, I don't have it. One night about two years after Dad's incident, I went into Corona for the evening. While I was there, I guess I talked too much—more than I should have. I know I mentioned having this collection to someone. Anyway, the next day a staff car came out to the ranch from Roswell with a captain and three enlisted men in it. Dad was away at the time; but it turned out they didn't want him anyway. They wanted me. Seems the captain—Armstrong, I think his name was, Captain Armstrong—had heard about my collection and asked to see it. Of course I showed it to him, and he said that this stuff was important to the country's security and that it was most important that I let him have it to take back with him. He seemed more interested in the string-like stuff than in any of the rest of it. I didn't know what else to do, so I agreed. Next he wanted me to take them out to the pasture where I had found this stuff. I said O.K. and took them there. After they had poked around a bit and satisfied themselves that there didn't appear to be any more of the material out there, the captain again asked me if I had any more of this material or if I knew of anyone else who did. I said no, I didn't; and he said that if I ever found any more that it was most important that I call him at Roswell right away. Naturally I said I would, but I never did because after that I never found any more.

Could this material have been part of a balloon of some sort?

No, I can answer that for sure. It was definitely not any kind of balloon. We've picked up balloons all over this

Bill Brazel, son of rancher W. W. Brazel. Bill's collection of "disc fragments" was confiscated by the Air Force in 1949 after Bill had "said too much" the evening before in a tavern in Corona, New Mexico.

(W. L. Moore)

country and any time we found one we always turned it in because there was sometimes a reward for them. This was no balloon, although I once asked Dad if he ever found anything like an instrument package connected with this stuff. He said no, there was no instrument package.

Strangely enough, when Dad first got into Roswell it was the weather bureau he called first about this stuff he had found. It was the weather bureau that told him he had better see the sheriff about it.

One more thing you might be interested in. One time I asked Dad whether there was any burned spot on the ground where this wreckage was. He said no, but that he had noticed on his second trip out there that some of the vegetation in the area seemed to have been singed a bit at the very tips—not burned, just singed. I don't recall seeing anything like that myself, but that's what he said.

Did your father ever mention anything about any creatures connected with this wreckage?

No, Dad never mentioned anything like that, but it's curious you should ask. There was a fellow who worked with me on a job in Alaska for a while who seemed to know something about that. We were talking about a number of things one evening and the topic of that flying saucer that was supposed to have touched down for a while on the Alaskan tundra came up. I mentioned to him about what Dad had been involved in, and to my surprise he asked me if I wanted to know more about that. Then he said that they had discovered the rest of that thing after it had come down in a desert area, and that there were some creatures found with it. He told me that when they had got inside of this wrecked saucer, that two of these creatures—he said they were about three and a half or four feet tall and bald—were still alive but that their throats had been badly burned from inhaling burning gases or fumes or something, and that they couldn't communicate. He said they were taken to California and kept alive on respirators for a period of time afterwards, but that both had died before we could figure out how to communicate effectively with them. This fellow's name was Lamme, and he told me the names of two other men who had been involved with this incident, but I can't recall what names they were right now. That's really all I can tell you on that one, except that it sure surprised me to hear such a story.

As we have already noted, Bill Brazel's father died in 1963, unfortunately without making any further statements to the press, and almost certainly without knowing anything about the little men to whom the wreckage he had found may have once belonged. Even so, in his years of silence, he must have had occasion to wonder why, if the incident really had cosmic importance, it was not later explained. He was certainly not the only one so to wonder.

Floyd Proctor was Brazel's closest neighbor. He lived about eight miles or so from the Brazel house, and when interviewed (Moore, June 1979) recalled the incident very well:

Brazel had come over to my place late one afternoon all excited about finding some sort of wreckage on his ranch. He wanted me to come over with him and look at it, and described it as "the strangest stuff he had ever seen." I was tired and busy and just didn't want to bother going all that way over there right then. You know he tried, he really tried to get us to go down there and look at it.

What did Brazel say about it?
He was in a talkative mood, which was rare for him, and just wouldn't shut up about it. He described the stuff

Photo taken on the Foster Ranch near Corona, New Mexico, showing the general area of the crash debris recovery site. Although an
apparent explosion on board the stricken saucer caused a large
quantity of debris and wreckage to fall here, the craft itself managed to remain in the air a while longer before crashing to earth
about 125 miles west of this site.

(W. L. Moore)

as being very odd. He said whatever the junk was, it had
designs on it that reminded him of Chinese and Japanese
designs. It wasn't paper because he couldn't cut it with his
knife, and the metal was different from anything he had
ever seen. He said the designs looked like the kind of stuff
you would find on firecracker wrappers . . . some sort of
figures all done up in pastels, but not writing like we
would do it.

Do you know what he did with it?
We suggested that he take it to Roswell . . . and the

next thing we knew he was in Roswell. They kept him
there about a week, under guard. He was real talkative
about that stuff until he came back; then he wouldn't say
much at all. He seemed to find something else to talk
about. He wouldn't say anything except that they had told
him it was some sort of balloon. Anyway, they kept Mac
down there several days and they sent a crew up here and
hauled everything away. Then they brought Brazel back on
a plane.

Did he say anything more about his stay on the base?

I don't know what they did to him down there in
Roswell, but I do know that L. D. Sparks [a former
neighbor] and I saw him down there in Roswell when we
were in town one time, and he was all surrounded by
military men, at least half a dozen, and walked right past
us like he didn't even know us.

When asked how many men came out to pick up the
pieces, Proctor said he didn't know. He said the location
of the crash site was seven and a half or eight miles from
the old Foster place (Brazel's ranch house—now torn down)
in a pasture used for sheep grazing. He said the land is
now occupied by a family named Chavez.

At about this point in the interview, Proctor's wife came
into the room and, after realizing what was being talked
about, volunteered some interesting information. Mrs. Proctor's brother, Robert R. Porter of Great Falls, Montana,
was one of the men on the plane that flew the wreckage to
Carswell AFB in Fort Worth on its way to Wright-Patterson
Field in Ohio. She recalls Porter saying that he had asked
several of the other men on the flight what all the secrecy
was about and whether the material they had under wraps
in the cargo hold was really a flying saucer. He was told:

"That's just what it is and don't ask any more questions."
He added that he didn't know for sure whether it was
Brazel's material or something else. Porter confirmed his
sister's account via a telephone interview in mid-July 1979
and also added that whatever was in the cargo hold was
escorted by an armed guard which had been assigned to it
at Roswell.

Brazel's elder sister, Lorraine Ferguson, lives in Capitan,
New Mexico, and, at the age of eighty-three, is an active
woman who has no trouble with her memory. When Moore
called on her in June 1979 she was hoeing the garden
alongside her house, wearing the large sunbonnet typical
of the "Old West." In a bit of preinterview reminiscence
she informed Moore that her father's first cousin was
Wayne Brazel—the man who killed Pat Garrett, who, for
his part, had already attained considerable fame for having
killed Billy the Kid.

QUESTION: *Why was William Brazel called Mac?*

We used to call him Mac because, when he was a baby,
he looked just like President McKinley.

*Do you remember a story about something crashing on
Mac's ranch at Corona?*

Sure, I remember, but Mac was extremely reluctant to
talk about it. He said he didn't want any great fuss about
it, but of course there was anyhow. Whatever he found it
was all in pieces and some of it had some kind of unusual
writing on it—Mac said it was like the kind of stuff you
find all over Japanese or Chinese firecrackers; not really
writing, just wiggles and such. Of course, he couldn't
read it and neither could anybody else as far as I ever
heard. . . . Everybody up there by the ranch knew about
it, but as far as I know nobody ever identified what it was

or what its purpose might have been. At first they called it a weather balloon, but of course it wasn't that. . . . Mac didn't ever like to be in the limelight, so he just naturally tried to avoid talking about it. Also, of course, the Air Force people had told him to be quiet too.

The unusual pictorial figures on the remnants of the foil, which, if part of a UFO, would be our first glimpse of extraterrestrial writing, again came up in a July 1979 interview with Bessie Brazel Schreiber, Mac Brazel's daughter.

Although she was only twelve years old at the time, the crash of a strange object on her father's ranch made a strong impression on her. She described the wreckage as "so much debris scattered over pastureland. There was what appeared to be pieces of heavily waxed paper and a sort of aluminum-like foil. Some of these pieces had something like numbers and lettering on them, but there were no words that we were able to make out. Some of the metal-foil pieces had a sort of tape stuck to them, and when these were held to the light they showed what looked like pastel flowers or designs. Even though the stuff looked like tape it could not be peeled off or removed at all. It was very light in weight but there sure was a lot of it."

QUESTION: *What happened when your father took some of this stuff into town to show the authorities?*

We were with him in Roswell but we didn't go with him to see these people. He went to the sheriff's department first and they sent him to the military. They talked to Dad all day. The following day we were descended upon by military people and news people. We were told not to talk about this at all. Back in those days when the military told you not to talk about something, it wasn't discussed.

Do you remember what this so-called writing looked like?

Yes. It looked like numbers mostly, at least I assumed them to be numbers. They were written out like you would write numbers in columns to do an addition problem. But they didn't look like the numbers we use at all. What gave me the idea they were numbers, I guess, was the way they were all ranged out in columns.

Could the object have been the remains of a weather balloon?

No, it was definitely not a balloon. We had seen weather balloons quite a lot—both on the ground and in the air. We had even found a couple of Japanese-style balloons that had come down in the area once. We had also picked up a couple of those thin rubber weather balloons with instrument packages. This was nothing like that. I have never seen anything resembling this sort of thing before—or since. . . . We never found any other pieces of it afterwards—after the military was there. Of course we were out there quite a lot over the years, but we never found so much as a shred. The military scraped it all up pretty well.

Finally, there is the question and sequence of Brazel's interview by KGFL Radio of Roswell, New Mexico. He was allegedly interviewed at the time of the incident on a wire recorder by W. E. Whitmore, then owner of KGFL, who planned to use the information as a ''scoop'' on the Mutual wire. W. E. Whitmore is now dead, but his son, Walt Whitmore, Jr., remembers that his father hid Brazel at the Whitmore home to keep the interview exclusive. At the very moment of the interview the Army, according to Whitmore, was ''having a fit'' because they could not locate the ''rancher who had found the flying saucer.'' Whitmore added that he did not know what happened to the rancher after he left the Whitmore home but assumed that the Air Force "caught up with him and put him out of circulation."

When Whitmore, Sr., had recorded the story and tried to get it on the Mutual wire, he was unable to get the call through. Meanwhile he began broadcasting a preliminary release locally over KGFL. At this point, however, a long-distance person-to-person phone call came through to the station from a man named Slowie, who identified himself as Secretary of the Federal Communications Commission in Washington, D.C. Slowie informed Whitmore, in a tone of voice that seemed to permit no further discussion, that the matter involved national security and that if Whitmore valued his FCC broadcasting license he would cease transmitting this story at once and forget that he had ever heard about it. While Whitmore, now concerned that he was onto something of cosmic importance, was trying to decide what to do next, a second call from Washington came through—this one from a senatorial level—from Senator Chavez of New Mexico, then chairman of the powerful Senate Appropriations Committee. Chavez suggested persuasively that Whitmore, Sr., had better do what Slowie advised and to obey the FCC directive. Whitmore complied with alacrity.

Whitmore, Jr., said that while he did not see the actual crash site until after the Army Air Force had "cleaned it up," he did see some of the wreckage brought into town by the rancher. His description was that it consisted mostly of a very thin but extremely tough metallic foil-like substance and some small beams that appeared to be either wood or wood-like. Some of this material had a sort of writing on it which looked like numbers that had been either added or multiplied. He recalls that his father went out to the site in a Buick but was turned back by armed

MPs who had set up a road block. Several other people from town tried to get out there but were stopped by guards, who told them that the area was blocked off because of a "Top Secret," project.

Several days later Whitmore, Jr., ventured out to the site and found a stretch of about 175-200 yards of pastureland uprooted in a sort of fan-like pattern with most of the damage at the narrowest part of the fan. He said that whatever it was "just cleaned it [the area] out. . . . The Army Air Force searched around out there for two days and cleaned out everything. I recall hearing that everything was taken to Wright-Patterson Air Force Base in Ohio after the Army Air Force had tried to piece the stuff together in Roswell. No one I talked to seemed to know exactly what it was, but I heard the 'flying saucer' explanation talked about quite a bit."

He added that the largest piece of this material that he saw was about four or five inches square, and that it was very much like lead foil in appearance but could not be torn or cut at all. It was extremely light in weight.

Walt Whitmore, Jr., remembers and sympathizes with Lieutenant Haut, then base I.O.: "The information officer out here at Walker [Roswell Army Air Base is now called Walker AFB] sure got his tail in a crack over this thing. He should never have released that story that they had picked up a saucer. He was here at the base for only a short time after that—matter of months maybe—and then they shipped him out."

Based on the information we have obtained thus far, we can postulate a tentative picture of the sequence of events and discovery. At between 9:45 and 9:50 P.M. on the evening of July 2, 1947, what appeared to be a flying saucer passed over Roswell heading northwest at a high rate of speed, as witnessed by the Wilmots. Somewhere north of Roswell, the saucer ran into the lightning storm witnessed by Brazel, made a course correction to the south-southwest, was struck by a lightning bolt, and suffered severe on-board damage. A great quantity of wreckage was blown out over the ground, but the saucer itself, although stricken, managed to remain in the air for at least long enough to get over the mountains before crashing violently to the ground in the area west of Socorro known as the Plains of San Agustin. The wreckage that had fallen on the Brazel ranch was discovered the next morning by Brazel as he was riding over his pasture, and only after that was Major Marcel of Roswell Army Air Base alerted. In the case of the saucer itself and its ill-fated crew, it had by chance come down near the spot where Barnett was scheduled to do a survey job the next morning and the archaeology students were scheduled to begin their dig.

At the second site on the Plains of San Agustin in Catron County, the military took over more quickly than at the first because of the delay involved between the time Brazel discovered the wreckage and the time he finally reported it to the authorities. Although the sequence of events at the San Agustin site had taken place several days before those at the Brazel ranch and in Roswell, news leaks from the San Agustin site were more effectively plugged and information coming in to media sources was slow to arrive and sketchy at best. As a result, even though this first military intervention did not come from the Roswell base, the early reports on the radio and in the press, in their confusion, assumed there was only one site and quite understandably referred only to the first site of the wreckage, which had received considerably more publicity because of Haut's premature news release. (One actually begins to wonder at this point whether Haut might have been ordered to leak the Roswell story to the press and write his news release specifically for the purpose of diverting attention away from the San Agustin incident.) In any event, indications are that the military group at the San Agustin site came from the air base at Alamogordo on the White Sands Proving Grounds, and that the secrecy involved here was far greater than at Roswell.

Even so, military communications were apparently working well at a high level, for a hastily assembled scientific-military expedition was, according to an alleged participant, sent to Muroc Air Base in California to meet the train which was to bring them the recovered wreckage and bodies (and possibly the two survivors as well).

This hastily assembled military-scientific group may have furnished the first approximate physical description of the occupants of the saucer and answered the question as to whether "they" were unlucky human test pilots or travelers from another world who had found their final destination on ours.

5

Descriptions of the Aliens

Meade Layne, now deceased, former director of Border-land Sciences Research Foundation, Vista, California, made some memos, probably in 1949, concerning reports on some of the alleged participants in this scientific "call-up." A memo has been furnished by Mr. Reilly Crabb, present director of Borderland Sciences Research Foundation.

Layne's memo states that "on the basis of present information" he accepted the facts of the story as authentic. Of his sources, he said that his "most direct information involves three informants, two of whom are scientists of distinction, and the third a business man of high standing.

One of the scientists, a Dr. Weisberg, a physics professor from a California university, saw the disc himself and took part in the examination of it. He says the disc was shaped like a turtle's back, with a cabin space some fifteen feet in diameter. The bodies of six occupants were seared . . . and the interior of the disc had been badly damaged by intense heat. One porthole had been shattered. . . .

An autopsy on one body showed that it resembled a normal human body except in size. One body was seated at what appeared to be a control desk, there were a few 'gadgets' in front of him, and on the walls or panels were characters in writing, in a language unknown to any of the investigators. They said it was unlike anything known to them, and was definitely not Russian. There was no propeller and no motor and they could not understand how it was driven or controlled. It was considered possible that the disc was wrecked by heat of friction with the atmosphere. . . .''

Dr. Weisberg's other testimony is especially interesting in that he suggests how the UFO got to its destination at Edwards Air Force Base. According to his recollection, it was taken by truck to Magdalena, in Guadalupe County, where it was put on a special car of the Atchison, Topeka and Santa Fe, which had been brought down from Vaughn. It was ''kept under wraps'' passing through Belen, Grants, and Gallup in New Mexico, Flagstaff, Arizona, to Needles and Cadiz in California and finally to Muroc, where Camp Edwards is located.

While we cannot be certain which material went to Fort Worth and which to Muroc, apparently shipments in both directions took place: the disc and its occupants to Muroc and the unusual wreckage to Fort Worth, and then on to Wright Field in Ohio. There are even persistent rumors that, sometime in the mid-1950s, presumably after an alleged viewing by President Eisenhower of the material and bodies at Edwards, they were reunited under one roof inside a structure referred to only as ''Building 18-A, Area B'' at Wright-Patterson Air Force Base. (Requests to Wright-

Patterson for information about the contents of Building 18-A are usually answered by the reply that there *is* no Building 18-A.) Later, again according to rumor, the Air Force in early 1978 reacted to increasing public pressure for disclosure by moving the carefully preserved bodies and some of the wreckage by Guppie aircraft to a specially constructed and guarded warehouse located on the CIA compound at Langley, Virginia. The remainder was shipped under heavy guard to McDill Air Force Base, Florida—where presumably it is still held, although not for public viewing.

A further and rather unusual type of corroboration that something significant was indeed recovered comes from the case of Baron Nicholas von Poppen, a Baltic German refugee nobleman from Estonia. Von Poppen had developed a system of photographic metallurgical analysis and was working in the Los Angeles area as an industrial photographer, concentrating primarily on the aircraft industry. According to statements quoted by Gray Barker (UFO *Report*, May 1977) a longtime investigator of UFOs and owner of the appropriately named Saucerian Press, Clarksburg, West Virginia, von Poppen was employed by military authorities to photograph the damaged saucer (by this time "flying saucer" had become part of current vocabulary).

The salient points of von Poppen's account are startling. On a certain unspecified date in the late 1940s, he was visited by two military intelligence representatives who offered him a top-secret photographic assignment at an exceptionally high fee, but with the proviso that he would immediately be deported if he revealed anything that he saw or photographed. Subsequently the agents escorted him by plane to an air base which, he was told, was Los Alamos (but which could have been Edwards since there was no air base at Los Alamos). He was taken to a large object which resembled the popular concept of a flying saucer. He stayed at the base for several days, photographing the object, his film being taken from the camera by military representatives as each film was completed. According to his recollection, he took hundreds of pictures. In the close-up shots he was told that it was important to show the texture of the metal.

Von Poppen thought that the machine was about thirty feet in diameter and the interior cabin about twenty feet in diameter with a curving ceiling. Between the inner cabin and the outside there was space for cables made of unfamiliar metals or alloys. In this main cabin there were four seats in front of a control board, which was "covered with push buttons and tiny levers." Plastic sheets covered with symbols lay scattered on the control board and on the floor.

Still strapped in each of the four seats was a dead body, extremely thin and varying in height from about two to four feet (a striking similarity to the extraterrestrials in *Close Encounters of the Third Kind*). As quoted by Gray Barker, von Poppen stated:

> The faces of all four were very white. . . . [They wore] shiny black attire, one-piece outfits without pockets and closely gathered at their feet and necks. . . . Their shoes . . . were made of the same material and appeared to be very soft—not rigid. . . . Their hands were human-like though soft, like those of children, complete with five digits, normal-looking joints, and neatly trimmed nails. . . .

As von Poppen had been employed to photograph metals and not extraterrestrials, he was discouraged from too

close examination of the surprising crew of the craft.
(Until he saw the occupants von Poppen had thought that
the craft, with its attendant high classification, had been a
top-secret air force project.)

As he continued for several days to photograph the
spaceship (but not the bodies) his scientific curiosity over-
came the warnings he had received about taking souvenirs.
He attempted to collect something from the craft, but was
later betrayed by a crucial beep at a checkpoint and as a
result was relieved of the object. Finally von Poppen was
taken back to Los Angeles by escort from the area identified as Los Alamos. Before he left he heard rumors that
the craft was to be transported to Wright-Patterson Air
Force Base in Ohio.

Although unsuccessful in separating any parts of the
craft for further study or further photography, von Poppen
was successful in hiding or later obtaining one print, a
view of the crashed saucer. He kept the negative in a
securely guarded envelope to be opened at the time of his
death or, as expressed in von Poppen's own guarded words,
"in case something should happen to me."

Von Poppen died in Hollywood in the summer of 1975
at the age of nearly ninety, but no trace of the photograph
in question has ever been found. If von Poppen secreted it
away in a safe-deposit box, then perhaps it reposes there
still, and if ever found by an unsuspecting bank official,
will doubtlessly not be recognized for what it is.

Len H. Stringfield is a longtime UFO investigator, the
author of *Situation Red, the UFO Siege* (Doubleday, 1977),
a researcher, and is director of public relations for Du Bois
Chemicals, Cincinnati, Ohio.

Stringfield, in an interview with Moore in July 1979,
stated that his son-in-law, Jeffry Sparks, an assistant professor of theater arts at St. Leo's College, Dade City,

Florida, had spoken with a person who claimed to have witnessed bodies of alien humanoid creatures at Wright-Patterson AFB sometime during 1966. Sparks relayed his contact's name to Stringfield, who subsequently spoke at length with this witness on July 5, 1978.

The individual involved, identified at his request because of security regulations as J.K., currently holds a responsible position with a private firm in Tampa, Florida. From 1966 to 1968, J.K. served as military intelligence officer with Nike Missile Air Intelligence (ADCAP) at Wright-Patterson.

While he was at Wright-Patterson, J.K. claims to have observed bodies of nine deceased aliens preserved under deep-freeze conditions in well-lighted, thick-glass enclosures. He described the bodies as short in stature, about four feet in height, and with what appeared under the lighting conditions to be a grayish skin. The research area where these bodies were preserved was constantly under heavy guard both inside and out.

While he was viewing the bodies, J.K. was told that there were no fewer than thirty such preserved at Wright-Patterson. Although he saw the bodies he did not actually see any alien craft at the base, but was informed that there were such craft there and also at Langley AFB and McDill AFB in Florida.

According to J.K., highly trained mobilized units are held at certain military bases in a constant ready state for dispatch to any area in the United States to recover downed or crashed UFOs. He also related that "since 1948 secret information concerning UFO activity involving the U.S. military has been contained in a computer center at Wright-Patterson" and that "duplicate support back-up files" are secretly kept at other selected military installations.

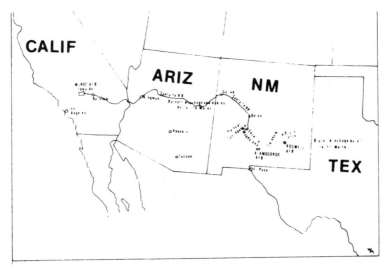

Possible military transport route of disc wreckage from crash site to Muroc Air Force Base, California.

(W. L. Moore)

The above statements are partially confirmed by Edward Gregory of Livermore, California, who worked on the P.R. staff at Roswell AAFB under Lieutenant Haut in 1947. (See Chapter 4.) Gregory eventually was transferred to the 3602d Squadron USAF whose assignment it was to investigate UFO reports for the Air Force, the reports going straight to Air Defense Command Headquarters. Gregory stated in a telephone interview with Stan Friedman that there were highly trained three-man teams ready to go at any time to any suspected UFO crash site. According to Gregory, during his time in the 3602d, these teams were called out several times on alleged UFO crashes.

Among many researchers of the Roswell Incident, Len Stringfield has been especially concerned about the physical appearance of the occupants of the so-called flying disc. He has been able, in the course of his investigations, to speak with doctors (unidentified at their urgent request) who were summoned by governmental agencies in the early fifties and employed in what was apparently a new series of autopsies, pursuant to whatever autopsies were made in 1947. One wonders why a new series of autopsies was called for: perhaps for comparison data or a renewal of interest in the alleged alien bodies, which, according to Stringfield, were kept in formaldehyde between autopsies— and still are. Further intensive research is being carried out in at least two major medical centers in the United States.

Stringfield reports incomplete overall information and opinions inasmuch as physicians with varying areas of specialization were utilized for different parts of the autopsy procedures. Thus no single source has more than a small portion of the relevant data at his disposal should he choose to break security to talk about it.

Certain information collected from several medical informants form a general impression of humanoid physical beings, partially described as follows:

Approximate height between three and a half and four and a half feet.

The head, by human standards, is oversize in relation to torso and limbs. Although brain capacity has not been specified it is considerably larger comparatively than that possessed by human beings.

Head and body are hairless although some report a slight fuzz on pate.

Eyes are large and deep-set or sunken, far apart, and slightly slanted.

No ear lobes or extending flesh beyond apertures noted on each side of the head.

Nose is formless, with nares indicated by only a slight protuberance.

Mouth is a small slit which may not function as an orifice for food ingestion. No mention of teeth was made by Stringfield's informants.

Neck is relatively thin.

Arms and legs are extremely thin, with arms reaching nearly to knee sections.

Hands show four fingers and no thumb, with two fingers double the length of the others. Fingernails are elongated. A slight webbing effect exists between the fingers.

Skin of tough texture and grayish. Skin on some preserved bodies appeared dark brown, evidently charred.

Blood is liquid but not similar to human blood by color or any known blood type.

There were conflicting reports on reproductive organs, with some observers reporting no distinguishing sex characteristics while others stated that there were

distinctive male and female bodies sexually comparable to those of human beings. (Although Barnett thought
all the bodies he saw were male.) Reports on internal
organs were not made available to Stringfield.

It seems fairly evident that incomplete reports such as
the above may have come from doctors who feared to say
too much or from laboratory attendants who did not have
sufficient information to give a more complete picture.
(One almost incomprehensible feature of an advanced technological race would be *four* fingers and no thumb, the
prehensile thumb being basically the principal physical
advantage over the animals—unless of course the first of
the four fingers was long and pliable enough to serve as a
thumb.) However, the description of the hand itself may
have represented an imperfect memory of a laboratory
assistant who saw the long fingers folded over the thumb
and counted only four. This at least is one possible explanation for the apparent discrepancy between Stringfield's
information and von Poppen's account of the aliens. It is
interesting to note that the aliens portrayed on board the
UFO in the film *Close Encounters of the Third Kind*
closely resemble the composite description compiled by
researcher Springfield. This is probably not an example of
"art imitating nature" but rather due to the fact that Dr. J.
Allen Hynek, Northwestern University astronomer and director of the Center for UFO Studies, a consultant on the
film, had access to various reports on the alleged characteristics of some examples of extraterrestrials.

In like manner, the subsequent "underground" reports
from high-security areas on the presence there and descriptions of the bodies of the saucer occupants as they were
shuttled from one military base to another around the
country, while differing in some particulars, nevertheless

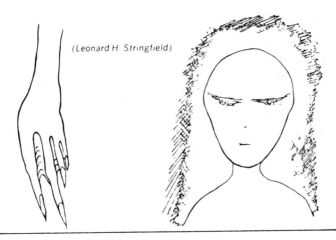

(Leonard H. Stringfield)

July 10, 1976

I hereby certify that I was shown a sketch of a
hand stated to be that of a retrieved humanoid
on July 13, 1978 in New York City. The sketch
was in the possession of Leonard Stringfield and
was the result of descriptions given him by
various confidential sources. I had not seen nor
discussed the sketch (or the humanoid material in
general) with Len prior to our meeting on July
13-14, 1978. Based on other sources known to me
and not to Len, the sketch appears identical to
material I have been familiar with for quite some
time. I had described the hands to my wife and
two close friends in late 1977 and they can
confirm the accuracy of the sketch as compared
with my description at that time. Based on my
somewhat limited knowledge, I must conclude that
the sketch is accurate.

Ted Phillips

Ted Phillips

Ted Phillips, of Sedalia, Missouri, specializes in the investigation of
UFO trace cases. He is affiliated with The Center for UFO Studies
and The Mutual UFO Network.

offer a description consistent enough to be considered fairly corroborative.

If the validity of the various descriptive reports is debatable one must still admit that the features of head enlargement, hairlessness, muscle deterioration, elongation of arms, loss of height, etc., might be said to be a perceptive guess of how *we* will look in the far future, the point from which the "aliens" may conceivably have come. It appears unlikely that the same stories should surface in so many places apparently unrelated except by the "journey in death" of the alien crew.

Alien from Another World, or Elaborate Hoax?
The authors publish this (unfortunately poor quality) photocopy and the accompanying artist's interpretation without comment about whether it may or may not pertain to certain significant aspects of the Roswell Incident. On May 22, 1950, an unnamed informant turned the original of this photograph over to agent John Quinn of the New Orleans FBI Field Office claiming he had purchased the photograph from another individual for the sum of $1.00 and was "placing it in the hands of the government" because it pictured "a man from Mars in the United States." The picture, which purports to show an alien survivor of a UFO crash in the custody of two U.S. military policemen, reportedly first surfaced in Wiesbaden, Germany, in the late 1940s allegedly in the possession of a U.S. GI stationed there at the time. How he came into possession of such a picture remains unclear, as do the identities of the two soldiers portrayed, the location of the military base where the picture was allegedly taken, and the exact nature of the portable respiratory apparatus that is obviously being used to assist the alien's breathing. The photo did receive limited publicity in West Germany in the late 1940s, although it was generally regarded with skepticism by U.S. officials of the then-existent Allied Military Government.

(Drawing by Lawrence Blazey, UFO Information Network [UFOIN], P.O. Box 5012, Rome, OH 44085)

6

Holes in the Cover-up

Despite the efforts of the AAF and thereafter the government to keep the entire matter (and their own research concerning the craft and its crew) under high-security classification, rumors have continued to surface throughout the years, sometimes from Edwards Air Force Base, sometimes from the Pentagon, or from Langley, Virginia (CIA headquarters). Some of these rumors come from security personnel who have been transferred to other duties or have retired and therefore tend to consider the matter with a mixture of nostalgia and permissiveness. The rumors sometimes corroborate and sometimes add new material.

Almost from the time of the original incident there has always been the expectation that disclosure of the mysterious events in Roswell would be made within a relatively short period of time. Norman Bean, Miami, Florida, electronics engineer, inventor, and lecturer on UFOs, remembers an incident that took place in the mid-fifties. After a lecture he had just given he had a conversation with a retired air force officer, a Colonel Lake, who informed him that a close friend had talked to a doctor in Dayton, Ohio, at some length about the autopsies of the "saucer" crew in which he had participated. According to Colonel Lake, the internal organs were similar to those of human beings, with basic organs "just like chickens and people." Colonel Lake, naturally aware of security regulations, said he could talk about this now in a general way because "all this is going to be a matter of public information in a few months."

Nothing, of course, has yet been officially disclosed. However, numerous lower-echelon disclosures have continued to surface, sometimes contradictory but in general agreement. These confidential disclosures usually come from military guards, personnel involved in the transportation of the bodies, doctors or autopsy assistants, clerks, and occasionally individuals unconnected with the project who somehow stumble on the not-so-secret secret.

A chance meeting on a train revealed some specific details, somewhat at odds with other descriptions of the aliens. Bill Devlin, an employee of a radio and television servicing company, en route in the spring of 1952 to Washington from Philadelphia, found a vacant seat next to a soldier who was reading a Philadelphia newspaper. Devlin was especially intrigued by an article the soldier was reading concerning a wave of UFO sightings over the Main Line of Philadelphia. Noting the interest of Devlin, who was reading over his shoulder, the soldier said: "This article here. I could tell you a lot more about this if you are interested." Upon assurance from Devlin that he was extremely interested, the soldier told him that he was one of three drivers who took the remains of a saucer from Aztec, New Mexico, to Fort Riley, Kansas, in a truck convoy consisting of three trucks. During the operation the soldier had seen the bodies and noted that they were very small, all dressed alike in close-fitting stretch garments, that they had human features (including teeth), and yellowish skin—somewhat "fuzzy," like a peach. They appeared to be male and female, as one of the figures "had bumps in the right places." He thought he counted "sixteen or so" small bodies, but did not know how many there actually were.

While such an account may seem somewhat unreliable at first glance, it may in fact be entirely accurate, although unfortunately we are forced to rely on rumor again as our best source of evidence. In this case, one crashed-saucer rumor that has circulated without appreciable change since the early 1950s has it that a small portion of the wreckage along with some of the bodies was transferred by truck convoy from Muroc to Wright Field about a year or so after the crash. According to this story, this was accomplished using three teams of drivers and escorts, each of which was responsible for moving the convoy only a part of the distance before turning their vehicles over to the next group at a specified rendezvous point. None of the groups knew anything specific about what they were carrying.

If this rumor is true, then several other seemingly incomprehensible pieces begin to fall into place. In the late 1940s, before the advent of interstate highways and high-powered trucks, it would have been likely that those responsible for the logistics of such an operation would have chosen a southern route to avoid the highest parts of the Rockies, and then charted a gradual northeasternly course across the Great Plains to Ohio. Is it possible that the rendezvous points along such a route were Aztec, New Mexico, Fort Riley, Kansas, and Godman Field, Kentucky? The four (counting Muroc) points are certainly about equidistant from one another and would, in the 1940s, have had the advantage of being along roads which were out of the way enough to avoid attracting undue attention. The final leg of the trip from Godman to Wright Field could easily have been accomplished by a special crew from Wright Field itself.

Yet another advantage to such a conjecture is that it offers a possible explanation of how Frank Scully, in his poorly researched 1950 book *Behind the Flying Saucers*, erroneously concluded that Aztec, New Mexico, had actually been the site of the crash. Of course, the rumor doesn't end here.

More rumors follow at Fort Riley. There an MP on sentry duty saw a delivery into a building, at which he had been assigned to guard duty, consisting of several wooden crates containing figures covered with sheets with what appeared to be dry ice on the top. The figures seemed to be about four feet long, maybe less. While he was on guard duty, a general entered with other officers and, according to the sentry, upon leaving told him to "shoot anyone [unauthorized] who tried to enter." The sentry did not know what the bodies were, but later heard in the barracks that they were the crew of the disc that had crashed in New Mexico.

There were a variety of reports from Edwards Air Force Base, all unattributed but quite persistent. It is interesting to note as a mark of the efficiency of security regulations that two of the informants were adamant not only in refusing the use of their names but even to having Edwards AFB *mentioned* lest their connection with the security force lead to their detection. One MP confided to a relative, and later to the author, that the bodies kept at Edwards were separated, some being kept "on ice" at Edwards and others sent to Washington for further dissection. A CID (Criminal Investigation Division) agent, in speaking of a "crashed UFO kept at Edwards," mentioned that a special technical research team studied the artifact for months but were unable to cut into the metal for purposes of examination and molecular or atomic identification.

A report from "an inside source" of what may be the "saucer's" latest stop, at CIA headquarters, Langley Field, Virginia, indicates that the crashed disc is still there and that "IBM is working on it and they can't figure out how it operates." As far as construction is concerned, it appears to be along the tongue-in-groove system rather than riveted and welded.

Another more detailed account of the presence at Wright-Patterson Air Force Base comes from a base civilian employee through Charles Wilhelm, a UFO investigator and contact of Len Stringfield. The one-time base employee, Mrs. Norma Gardner, had retired for health reasons in 1959 and was living alone in Price Hill, Cincinnati. Charles Wilhelm, then a teenager, had been working at odd repair and upkeep jobs for Mrs. Gardner and in the course of their acquaintance had spoken to her about his interest in UFOs, which he soon realized she shared.

When Mrs. Gardner's health worsened, Wilhelm continued to visit her. On one visit, according to Wilhelm, she confided to him some rather startling information about her own knowledge of salvaged UFOs and alien bodies at the base. She said that while she was working at Wright-Patterson in 1955, she had been assigned to a post which involved the cataloguing of all incoming UFO-related material. She was given a top security clearance and, in the course of her duties, processed over 1,000 separate items, including parts from the interior of a recovered UFO which had been brought to the air base some time in the past. All items, she said, had been carefully photographed and tagged. In 1955 she visited an off-limits hangar and saw two saucer-like craft, one apparently intact and the other damaged.

At one point during the course of her assignment, she said, she had witnessed the conveyance of two humanoid bodies by cart from one room to another. She not only saw the bodies but personally handled the paper work on their autopsy reports. These bodies, preserved in some type of chemical solution, were between four and five feet tall, with generally human-like features except that the heads were large relative to the bodies and the eyes were slanted. She did not know whether the bodies had been brought in from a recent crash or had been on the base from some previous incident.

Mrs. Gardner told Wilhelm of her experiences when she was bedridden with cancer. So convinced was she that she would not recover that she apparently had second thoughts about security regulations, observing dramatically, "Uncle Sam can't do anything to me when I'm in my grave."

Among the more startling of the many rumors concerning the crashed disc is the one that suggests that the object was brought down by air force action, perhaps accidentally, through radar interference with the operational technology of the disc.

The above supposition, however, would seem to be negated by the many air force and FAA reports of instances when a good radar UFO lock-on failed to modify its flight plan and/or the distressing ability of UFOs simply to disappear, as if passing swiftly into another dimension where radar cannot follow them.

In 1956 an RB-47 reconnaissance plane, especially equipped with electronic radar gear, was followed by a

UFO for more than an hour over the Gulf of Mexico, Mississippi, Louisiana, Texas, and finally Oklahoma before it finally disappeared. If radar could affect the operation of UFOs, this would have been a case in point, unless, of course, more recent UFOs possess counterdevices.

The concept of challenge, combat, or conquest, certainly a consideration always present on an earthly level, has naturally been extended by earthly thinkers to UFOs and their possible intentions. For this reason it is relatively easy for one to explain the increasingly numerous sightings of UFOs from 1947 on, and, too, extraterrestrial curiosity about what was going on at White Sands and how far the denizens of a relatively minor planet were progressing in unleashing, for good or bad, the latent powers of the universe.

It seems unlikely, therefore, that the Roswell UFO was brought down, either accidentally or on purpose, by any activity of our military forces. Far more likely is the conjecture that the disc was struck by a lightning bolt, as seems to be indicated in Brazel's story. The speed with which the Army Air Force arrived on the scene of the San Agustin wreckage can easily be explained by the fact that either White Sands radar or a military or commercial aircraft in flight could have spotted the object going down the night before and naturally assumed it was some conventional craft out of control and suffering communication difficulties. The first military men on the scene could very well have been nothing more than part of a search and rescue team directed to the site by an aircraft spotter. When they realized what they had found, the news began, like the waves from a stone dropped into a pond, rapidly to increase in area, from the base to the state, the nation, and the world, until a command decision was taken to establish that nothing unusual had happened at all.

But the above selection of credible and incredible rumors, scuttlebutt, "confidential" reports, and twice-told tales, fantastic though they may seem, often corroborate the original precensorship radio and press reports as well as the testimony of on-the-spot witnesses. In any case they kept the crashed-saucer incident very much alive for years. By 1954, therefore, seven years after the reputed occurrence, they attracted the attention of someone in what may be termed a position of "supreme power." He assuredly had enough power, in any case, to do something about it. This person was Dwight Eisenhower, President of the United States.

7

The President and the Captured Saucer

Doubtlessly because of his military background, General Eisenhower was probably more aware of the importance of chance intelligence than other Presidents of this era (who, although having had military experience, were not military careerists), more interested in intelligence of a military potential, and certainly better able to evaluate it. During his first term as President, Eisenhower began to make inquiries into the reality of the "Roswell saucer capture."

One of his first problems, as outlined by a former high-level CIA operative who shall remain nameless, was his startling (one might even say frightening) discovery that even though he was President, as well as a former general of the Army, he did not possess the necessary clearances to be permitted access to such information. The intelligence agencies of the time were then enjoying a period of action untrammeled by the supervision or excessive curiosity of other agencies and certain classified and sensitive information might be secured for a time from even the President. According to an understandably anonymous source: ''Some of the higher-ups in the intelligence community didn't trust Ike and were hesitant to deal with him. These people frequently went off on their own tangents at that point in time and either conveniently forgot to seek directives from the White House, or ignored them when they did come.''

Eisenhower, however, eventually learned of the rumors of the allegedly crashed saucer and proceeded to take some action. Not surprisingly, according to sources as close to the topic as we can get, he reportedly encountered a split within the military establishment on this matter. We can imagine the reasoning among opponents of declassification: it would be advisable to keep the saucer incident silent—it is supremely important not just for scientific interest in extraterrestrials but for national security. Any nation that could figure out how the discs operated and could duplicate their maneuverability would have a missile defense and delivery system inestimably in advance of the systems presently developed or even logically contemplated and would therefore be in a position to control the planet earth.

Taking this into consideration, the reticence of military authorities to admit the actuality of the Roswell Incident and, in general, the automatic downgrading of UFO sightings become more understandable. One favorite theory for censorship has been: if the public were advised of a concrete proof of the real presence of UFOs they would panic. But whether the public would panic or not is unpredictable. Perhaps a serious and cooperative interest on the part of the public toward UFOs would be beneficial; certainly we would learn more about them. On the other hand, if the UFOs represent a definite military advantage, then they should be kept secret until their construction and operation could be adapted to the advantage of one world power, preferably ours. This reasoning may be why the superpowers employ strict censorship re UFOs while other countries with efficient air forces and surface fleets frequently release official reports concerning UFO encounters in the skies and at sea by their air and surface craft patrols. These countries include, among others, Argentina, Chile, Uruguay, Colombia, Mexico, Spain, Italy, Sweden, Norway, Australia, New Zealand, and, to an increasing degree, Canada.

Canada's connection with the UFO question has long been intensified by its proximity to the U.S.A., an area of so much apparently "extraterrestrial" activity, and also by the increasingly reported presence of UFOs, which perhaps do not recognize international boundaries, over its own immense territory. A memo addressed to the Department of Transport, Ottawa, dated November 21, 1950, from a W. B. Smith, indicates the Canadian interest in the U.S. Government's preoccupation with UFOs that began shortly after the incident at Roswell.

Wilbert B. Smith, as senior radio engineer of the Department of Transport and head of that department's Broadcast and Measurements Section, was evidently designated to be one of the Canadian representatives to a 1950 National Association of Radio Broadcasting (NARB) conference in Washington, D.C. Smith was particularly interested in research concerning the possibility of developing power sources utilizing the earth's own magnetic field.

Pertinent parts of this formerly "Top Secret" memo (downgraded to "Confidential" September 15, 1969) follow:

Memorandum to the Comptroller of Telecommunications
. . . We believe that we are on the track of something which may well prove to be the introduction to a

new technology. The existence of a different technology is borne out by the investigations which are being carried on at the present time in relation to flying saucers. . . .

While in Washington attending the NARB conference, two books were released: one entitled *Behind the Flying Saucers* by Scully and the other *The Flying Saucers Are Real* by Don Keyhoe. Both books dealt mostly with the sightings of UFOs and both claim that the flying objects were of extraterrestrial origin and might well be space ships from other planets.

It appeared to me that our own work in geomagnetics might be aided by U.S. intelligence information on UFOs.

I made discreet inquiries through the Canadian Embassy staff who were able to obtain for me the following information.

(a) The matter is the most highly classified subject in the U.S. government, rating higher even than the H-bomb. [*Author's note:* The H-bomb still had two years to go, as it was first exploded in 1952.]
(b) Flying saucers exist.
(c) Their modus operandi is unknown but concentrated effort is being made by a small group headed by Dr. Vannevar Bush.
(d) The entire matter is considered by the U.S. authorities to be of tremendous significance.

Particularly relevant to this memo is a letter attached to it dated September 15, 1969, authorizing the downgrading of classification from "Top Secret" to "Confidential," and stating that "at no time should [this information] be made available to the public.''

President Eisenhower, doubtlessly perplexed by the UFO furor in government circles occurring in the United States at this time, would certainly, as a military officer experienced in assessing intelligence reports, have had a particular interest in determining the truth of the concrete presence of the legendary captured saucer at Edwards Air Force Base. According to a series of reports, including one rather detailed account, he had a chance to examine it firsthand at Muroc on February 20, 1954.

He had gone to California in the middle of February for a golfing vacation during which he was staying at the ranch of a friend, Paul Roy Helms. For theorists who postulate that Ike's vacation in California was a cover for a secret visit to Muroc, it is interesting to observe that the President had just come back from a quail-shooting vacation in Georgia less than a week before. It can also be noted that Muroc is not very far from Palm Springs, where the President was staying, and a visit to Muroc would have been possible if he could have disappeared from the press corps' constant scrutiny for even one day.

On February 20, Eisenhower apparently went somewhere on his own, without his entourage, and, for the press corps at least, he had disappeared. Late in the evening of the twentieth, wild rumors began to circulate among the press corps to the effect that the President was not where he was supposed to be—that he had either disappeared from the ranch, Smoke Tree, or something very serious had happened to him.

With repeated phone calls to official sources at the ranch bringing only repeated assurances that all was well, the reporters were left free to speculate. The tension of an already shaky situation was heightened when several reporters succeeded in wringing from confidential sources that the President really was missing, but when word arrived that Press Secretary James Haggerty had been hastily summoned to Smoke Tree from the midst of a steak cook-out to make a statement, the pent-up speculation of the press corps ran amok.

Where, in fact, was the President? Nobody seemed to know for sure. Merriman Smith of the United Press, jumping to the hasty conclusion that Eisenhower had suffered a medical emergency of some sort, hit the press wire with a report that the President had been taken from the ranch for "medical treatment." The Associated Press did him one better by flashing on its New York wire the news that Ike was dead, only to be forced to retract it moments later when Press Secretary Haggerty appeared, definitely not in a good mood.

In the press room of the Mirador Hotel, amid a scene described by *Time* magazine as a "demonstration of journalistic mob hysteria," Haggerty solemnly announced that the uproar had in fact been caused by nothing more than the President having "knocked a cap off a tooth" while chewing on a chicken leg, and that he had been taken by his host, Paul Helms, to a local dentist, to have it repaired.

The press corps accepted the story, but the rumors persisted. Had Ike really gone to a local dentist, or was the story a cleverly concocted cover for what had really happened? At least one persistent (although generally discredited) rumor had it that there were other reasons for Ike's disappearance that evening—and the reason was somewhat "out of this world." According to this new rumor, the President's tooth was all a cover story, and that in fact he had been taken, in strictest secrecy, to nearby Edwards Air Force Base to view the remains of the crashed disc(s) and the preserved bodies of the little men that had piloted it (them).

Meade Layne, then director of Borderland Sciences Research Associates (now Borderland Sciences Research Foundation, see Chapter 5), had heard these rumors too, but had paid little attention to them until about three months later when, on April 16, 1954, he received a startling letter from one of his associates, Gerald Light of Los Angeles. In this letter Light stated that he had spent some forty-eight hours at Edwards Air Force Base in the company of three other men—journalist Franklin Allen of the Hearst newspapers, financier Edwin Nourse of the Brookings Institute, and Bishop (later Cardinal) James F. A. McIntyre of Los Angeles—and had seen no fewer than "five separate and distinct types of aircraft being studied" by military scientists and officials. Light said he was so shaken by what he had seen that he qualified his reactions as giving him "the distinct feeling that the world had come to an end with fantastic realism." No wonder! The letter follows:

GERALD LIGHT
10545 Scenario Lane
Los Angeles, California

[Letter Received
4-16-54]

Mr. Meade Layne
San Diego, California

My dear Friend: I have just returned from Muroc. The report is true—devastatingly true!

I made the journey in company with Franklin Allen of the Hearst papers and Edwin Nourse of Brookings

Institute (Truman's erstwhile financial adviser) and Bishop MacIntyre [*sic*] of L.A. (confidential names, for the present, please.)

When we were allowed to enter the restricted section, (after about six hours in which we were checked on every possible item, event, incident and aspect of our personal and public lives) I had the distinct feeling that the world had come to an end with fantastic realism. For I have never seen so many human beings in a state of complete collapse and confusion as they realized that their own world had indeed ended with such finality as to beggar description. The reality of "otherplane" aeroforms is now and forever removed from the realms of speculation and made a rather painful part of the consciousness of every responsible scientific and political group.

During my two days visit I saw five separate and distinct types of aircraft being studied and handled by our air-force officials—with the assistance and permission of The Etherians! I have no words to express my reactions.

It has finally happened. It is now a matter of history.

President Eisenhower, as you may already know, was spirited over to Muroc one night during his visit to Palm Springs recently. And it is my conviction that he will ignore the terrific conflict between the various "authorities" and go directly to the people via radio and television—if the impasse continues much longer. From what I could gather, an official statement to the country is being prepared for delivery about the middle of May. I will leave it to your own excellent powers of deduction to construct a fitting picture of the mental and emotional pandemonium that is now shattering the consciousness of hundreds of our scientific ''authorities'' and all the pundits of the various specialized knowledges that make up our current physics. In some instances I could not stifle a wave of pity that arose in my own being as I watched the pathetic bewilderment of rather brilliant brains struggling to make some sort of rational explanation which would enable them to retain their familiar theories and concepts. And I thanked my own destiny for having long ago pushed me into the metaphysical woods and compelled me to find my way out. To watch strong minds cringe before totally irreconcilable aspects of ''science'' is not a pleasant thing. I had forgotten how commonplace such things as the dematerialization of ''solid'' objects had become to my own mind. The coming and going of an etheric, or spirit, body has been so familiar to me these many years I had just forgotten that such a manifestation could snap the mental balance of a man not so conditioned. I shall never forget those forty-eight hours at Muroc!

G.L.

Assuming that this letter is not a hoax, there are several key points which seem to emerge as one examines it—not the least of which is the question of who this Gerald Light might be and what he was doing at Edwards with the three reasonably well-known figures he names. Unfortunately almost nothing is known about Light himself aside from the fact that Meade Layne, recipient of the letter, described him once in an early BSRF publication as a ''gifted and highly educated . . . writer and lecturer'' who liked to dabble in clairvoyance and the occult. Additional research has turned up the fact that there was a Gerald Light employed in the early 1950s as director of advertising and sales promotion of CBS Columbia—the manufacturing division of the Columbia Broadcasting System. But whether this was the same man remains unclear. Reilly Crabb, current director of BSRF, could provide no further information except to say that he had heard that Light had died some years ago. As for the other three men named, Crabb told me he knew of several attempts which had been made over the years to contact these people about Gerald Light's story, but that none of them would discuss the matter or even acknowledge receipt of letters concerning it. Since Allen, Nourse, and Cardinal McIntyre are now dead, the mystery may never be solved.

The most interesting thing about Light's letter, however, is his assertion that "President Eisenhower . . . was spirited over to Muroc *one night during his visit to Palm Springs recently"*—an assertion at variance with Press Secretary Haggerty's "chicken bone" explanation for Ike's disappearance on the night of February 20.

If, indeed, Eisenhower had only been taken to the dentist, then why the long official silence on the matter and the repeated statements from Smoke Tree that all was well? If the dentist story were true, it would certainly have been a case where the truth could have been told and the wild rumors circulating about Ike's disappearance quelled at once without having done any harm in the process. The attempted "all is well" cover-up at first and then the calling of Haggerty himself to deal with what must have appeared as a mounting crisis with the press seems excessive for the simple explanation that followed. Admittedly the evidence is circumstantial at best, but it is nonetheless interesting.

One certain thing about Light's letter is the fact that his

conviction about Eisenhower being prepared to "go directly to the people . . . about the middle of May" definitely never came to pass. If Ike was preparing an official statement on the matter, he must have been persuaded not to deliver it by those same "authorities" that had been advocates of strict secrecy from the very beginning. Apparently Ike was let in on the secret as one of the first of a small but carefully selected group of scientific, military, and civilian personnel from all walks of life (Light, Allen, Nourse, and McIntyre must also have been selected as part of this group) who were shown the evidence over a period of time—possibly for the purpose of gauging from their observed reactions what the effect on the general public would likely be if such a story were released. If such is the case, the mental confusion and near pandemonium that appear to have resulted and that Light describes in his letter must have provided enough ammunition to result in a total victory for the forces of secrecy. The witnesses who had seen the evidence were silenced on their oaths and the project to release the news to the public was resultantly scrapped. (Eisenhower, it is said, ordered silence and further study.) The fact that Gerald Light apparently broke his oath by writing to Meade Layne probably left them unperturbed once it was discovered that Layne was not important enough to make the story stick even if he did publish it.

Another interesting piece of information on the presence of saucer-crash wreckage at Edwards comes from the late British saucer researcher and writer Desmond Leslie, who reportedly did some investigating in the Muroc vicinity while on a visit to Los Angeles during the summer of 1954. Leslie told writer George Hunt Williamson in an interview for *Valor* magazine on October 9, 1954, that "discreet inquiries" had convinced him that the "rumored saucer at Muroc was actually there'' and that it was being kept under guard ''in hangar 27.'' According to Leslie, ''President Eisenhower had a 'look-see' at the craft during his Palm Springs vacation.'' He would identify his source of information only as ''an Air Force man'' who had actually ''seen the craft,'' and who had told him that ''on a certain day . . . suddenly men coming back from leave were not allowed to go back on the base and were given orders to 'get lost.' '' Others, said his informant, had such personal belongings as they needed brought to them as they waited at the gate. Men who were stationed at the base that day were not allowed to leave under any circumstances.

Unfortunately, Leslie had previously compromised his reliability through an association with the late George Adamski, reputed saucer contactee of the 1950s and an individual long associated with the so-called lunatic fringe of UFOlogy. Even though Leslie's story may well have been true, few at the time were willing to believe it.

Two other bits of research, however, have since come to light which seem to indicate that there may be some truth here after all. The first deals with the dentist who was supposed to have treated Ike for his broken tooth. Although the dentist is now dead, Moore succeeded in contacting a member of his family in June 1979 and found her strangely reluctant to talk about the incident. While she said she did recall the dentist's being called upon to treat the President, she was curiously unable to remember what time of day it was, what the circumstances were surrounding the event, what the President's problem was, or even how many times he saw the dentist (''I can't recall how many times—maybe twice, maybe more. I don't remember.'') She did recall, however, attending ''a presidential steak-fry'' the next evening where he was loudly introduced to reporters as "the dentist who had treated the President."

It would seem that a family member of anyone, doctor or dentist, called out in midevening to treat the President of the United States for an "emergency" would more vividly recall the details of the incident, even after twenty-five years.

In summary, the very fact that she "cannot recall" details which most people under similar circumstances would easily remember seems strongly to suggest that the extent of the dentist's involvement was only to act as a convenient (howbeit willing) accessory to the cover story worked up by Press Secretary Haggerty to placate the press corps. While the family may have viewed the entire matter as a part of their patriotic duty at the time, it seems natural that now, twenty-five years after the fact, a family member is unable to recall the details of what she was told to tell reporters at the time. Her embarrassment at this could easily explain her reluctance to have her name connected with it.

Another relevant bit comes from Mrs. Frank Scully, widow of the author of *Behind the Flying Saucer* (Chapter 3), who recalled that in 1954 she and her husband had bought a cabin in the desert mountains above Edwards Air Force Base. According to Mrs. Scully, one of the carpenters who came to work for them in about June of that year had previously worked as a civilian employee at Edwards. This man, whose name she was unable to recall, had told them that Eisenhower had indeed visited the base in secrecy some months before, and that it was strange the press had never learned about it.

Perhaps some members of the press did learn about it, but were unable to confirm it and so kept silent. Captain Edward J. Ruppelt, who at the time had just recently

(September 1953) stepped down as head of the Air Force's UFO Project Blue Book, had also heard the rumors it seems, and was interested enough in them to take the trouble to compose a type-written memo on the topic. Although this memo, which was discovered by Moore during an examination of the Ruppelt files many years after his death, unfortunately gives no indication as to whether Ruppelt believed the story or not, its very presence allows us to infer that Ruppelt must have had more than just a passing interest in the topic.

More recently, a former high-level member in one of the departments under Eisenhower, now living in Arizona, has confirmed privately to friends that Ike did indeed visit Muroc in 1954 to see the remains of the crashed disc and the bodies, and that the trip had been made from Palm Springs by helicopter.

What happened to the disc after Eisenhower's visit? All we have to go on is rumor and circumstance; but some of these imply that in late 1954 (due perhaps to the publicity mentioned above) the disc was partially dismantled and shipped by low-boy truck to Wright-Patterson Air Force Base in Dayton, Ohio, to join the bits of wreckage and bodies which had preceded them there in the late 1940s.

But prior to General Eisenhower's visit certain unusual happenings had been noted in the skies over the area of Muroc. A number of UFO sightings in the area before the objects and bodies were reportedly moved include the following:

July 8, 1947: Four separate sightings of unidentified disc-shaped objects were observed over Muroc Air Force Base and Rogers Dry Lake secret testing site in California. One object passed over above an F-51 aircraft at a time when no known aircraft was in the vicinity.

August 31, 1948: Large unknown object trailing blue flame exhaust nearly one mile long was reported cruising at 50,000 feet above U.S. Air Force Base at Muroc. Civilian pilot Bob Hanley and two passengers reported seeing the same or similar object over Mint Canyon at 12:15 A.M.

June 24, 1950: Navy transport pilot and crew and several airline pilots watched cigar-shaped object maneuvering above Mojave Desert near Daggett, California, about twenty-five miles east of Muroc Air Force Base. Object paced United Airlines commercial flight for nearly twenty miles.

August 10, 1950: Naval physicist Lieutenant Robert C. Wykoff observed large disc-shaped object through Navy 7 x 50 calibrated binoculars as it maneuvered between himself and a distant range of hills. Sighting occurred along U.S. Route 395 near Edwards, about ten miles north of the junction of old U.S. Route 466.

September 30, 1952: Dick Beemer, aviation photographer, and two other witnesses observed a pair of flattened, spherical-shaped objects hovering, maneuvering and performing sharp turns over Edwards Air Force Base.

In this connection it may be pertinent to note that Nicholas von Poppen, the photographer who said that he took photographs of the crashed UFO (and saw some dead crew members) at "Los Alamos," noted that at the time of his visit the base was in a state of alert as a precautionary measure should other UFOs suddenly appear on a rescue or retrieval mission. Besides a desire to obtain information on the part of UFO investigators and perhaps President Eisenhower, there may have existed (and may still exist) a certain interest from intelligences from beyond this planet.

A prevalent rumor in UFO circles about the Roswell Incident revolves around another leading figure in the United States Government, Senator Barry Goldwater of Arizona. This rumor concerns an alleged attempt on the part of Senator Goldwater (who holds the rank of general in the United States Air Force) to visit a high-security area at Wright-Patterson Air Base, where, according to rumor the Roswell UFO as well as the bodies of the dead extraterrestrial crew were then kept, and being refused admittance on a "need to know" basis.

According to Senator Goldwater, what actually happened was the following: while en route to California in the early 1960s, the senator stopped at Wright-Patterson Air Base, where he visited his friend General Curtis LeMay. Senator Goldwater had heard of the existence of a room or section on the base referred to as "Blue Room," where UFO artifacts, photographs, and exhibits were kept. The senator, who, as a longtime pilot, had more than a passing interest in UFOs, requested permission from General LeMay to visit the Blue Room exhibits. General LeMay's response was eminently succinct: "Hell, no. I can't go, you can't go, and don't ever ask me again!"

Although unable to view what to most researchers would have been conclusive proof of the existence of extraterrestrial flying objects, Senator Goldwater's reflections on the possibility of extraterrestrial life and probable technological development have been expressed by him in what might be termed a guideline for cosmic speculation: "I cannot believe that we are the only planet where there are sentient beings. . . . I have every reason to believe that other beings from other parts of the universe are as smart or smarter than we are. . . ."

Perhaps the Blue Room contained an answer. But whatever *was* inside was evidently regarded as so secret that it could not be visited even by top air force generals.

8

"Top Secret" Forever— the AVRO Alternative

If the United States Government actually did manage to pick up enough pieces of the Roswell object roughly to determine what it was and something of how it operated, it would therefore be understandable that it would be treated as "Top Secret" during the life of existing security regulations. This would seem to be especially necessary since an increasing number of foreign nations would wish to obtain what could perhaps be the ultimate secret weapon. Then again, perhaps other UFOs had already crashed or might crash in other parts of the world and other nations would be in possession of other parts of a cosmic jigsaw puzzle whose successful solution would give the nation in question the secret of flight at incredible velocity and without the use of fuels as we presently conceive them.

The results of recovery operations would therefore have to be studied under conditions of strict security and actually to fly such devices. These attempts, in turn, have subsequently generated their own crop of rumors. One fairly prevalent rumor of such an experiment has been reported by Reilly Crabb, president of the Borderland Science Research Foundation of Vista, California.

Crabb learned about the alleged incident from an air force sergeant in 1971 who told Crabb that it happened four years previously while he was on temporary duty at Edwards Air Force Base. During his time there the sergeant had become friendly with a certain fighter pilot whom he refused to name but whom he described as being the "Steve Canyon" type. In a conversation with "Canyon" one day within one of the hangars they discussed the topic of UFOs and the sergeant expressed his interest and belief in the phenomenon. The officer listened for a few moments, hesitated, and suddenly said: "I want to show you something. Just follow me and don't ask questions. I won't answer them anyway."

The sergeant was led to another hangar "where security precautions were not so stringent but that his uniform and ID card got him into the side office and shop area." The two proceeded to an upper level where there were offices with side windows overlooking the hangar floor below— all of which were heavily curtained. On the floor ahead was a red line beyond which a guard would let no one pass without proper authorization. The pilot whispered to the sergeant to wait for him there and, while waiting, to catch a look through a slightly parted curtain behind him at what was on the hangar deck directly below.

The pilot went on through security and, since the guard seemed unconcerned, the sergeant took what he described to Crabb as a "good look." What he saw was a "saucer-shaped craft sitting on high landing gear. It was completely circular with sharp edges sloping up to a domed cockpit area in the center. It looked as if it were capable of carrying at least two, perhaps three, persons, and [was] probably twenty-five to thirty feet in diameter overall.'' There were service personnel dressed in the usual air-force-blue coveralls moving around the craft as it sat there.

The pilot soon returned and the sergeant followed him out of the area. Just before they parted, the pilot reminded him to say nothing about what he had seen or where he had been, and that if he did, he (the pilot) would deny it all.

''Do you think that was a flying saucer built and operated by U.S. Air Force personnel?'' asked Crabb.

''I do,'' replied the sergeant. ''In fact, I became acquainted with civilian guards there at Edwards who claimed to have seen these disc-shaped craft operating from specially camouflaged hangars at night.''

Reilly Crabb's informant transferred to Vietnam shortly after their conversation where, Crabb believes, he met his death in action.

In seeming confirmation of the likelihood that at least some governmental research has been carried out on a saucer-like disc-shaped craft is a persistent rumor that such an object was indeed test-flown over Nellis AFB in Nevada during 1965, stored for a period of time, and then test-flown again, presumably with some additional modifications, in 1974. Some informants claim to have seen such a plane, referred to as the ''Flying Flapjack,'' in a commercial newsreel. When one such witness wrote the TV program *You Asked For It* and requested a rerun of the newsreel on TV, he was informed that the newsreel had been acquired by the government and was henceforth ''Top Secret.'' The Flying Flapjack has been a dead project (officially) since the 1940s, and, presumably, the only aircraft of this type ever built never left Connecticut.

When asked by letter about such a rumor, the Air Force

invariably refers the inquirer to the nonclassified and highly visible work done by the Air Force between 1954 and 1959 in contract with the A. V. Roe Ltd. aeronautics firm of Toronto. Some $10 million was spent to develop the so-called AV-9 AVRO car disc-shaped aircraft—a monumental flop which never got more than a few feet off the ground and wobbled like a Yo-Yo when it finally was test-flown in December 1959. This technological disaster, according to the Air Force, is as far as anyone has ever progressed in trying to force the saucer shape to conform to the principles of aerodynamics. The case would seem to be closed.

Or is it? For recently some of those connected with the AVRO project have suggested otherwise—have suggested that the ill-fated AVRO car was really nothing more than a monumental blind designed to divert public attention from the real research going on with actual "captured" hardware or attempts at duplicating it. Lieutenant Colonel George Edwards, USAF (Ret.) of New York, a scientist who lays claim to actually having been involved in the AVRO VZ-9 manmade saucer project, had gone on record *(Ideal's UFO Magazine,* No. 4, Fall, 1978) as saying that he and others involved with the project knew from the beginning that it would never succeed and that the VZ-9 would never fly. "Although we weren't cut in on it," he is quoted as saying, "we know that the AF was secretly test-flying a real alien spacecraft. The VZ-9 was to be a 'cover,' so the Pentagon would have an explanation whenever people reported seeing a saucer in flight." If the above were true (and the VZ-9 was certainly itself a fact) this could be classified as one more example of "gray" propaganda as described on page 54.

The mystery of the crashed disc or UFO near Roswell at the very beginning of the "UFO age" will probably be revealed only when governmental authorities release the mountains of UFO information they have been collecting through the years. The quest for information by interested civilians is complicated not only because pertinent agencies have been unwilling to release information but also because UFO reports are not concentrated in any one agency. They are variously held by the CIA, the FBI, NASA, the Air Force, the Navy, the National Security Agency, and the National Archives, among others, and, as could be expected, reports have been lost or misfiled while on loan to another agency.

UFO groups have been agitating and lobbying to this effect since the 1960s but now, because of the passage of the amended Freedom of Information Act (5USC-552), which took effect appropriately on July 4, 1974, the logjam of withheld information seems to be giving some signs of breaking up.

The Freedom of Information Act détente was accompanied by optimistic portents. Carter, in his presidential campaign, stated that he had personally seen a UFO in Georgia while he was governor and that he would release government-held UFO information if elected President, providing the release of such information did not compromise the nation's security interests.* In April 1977, *U.S. News & World Report* prophesied: before the year is out the government—perhaps the President—is expected to make what are described as "unsettling disclosures" about

---

*A request for information re releasing UFO reports was directed to President Carter by the authors in 1979 because of inquiries they had received in this matter from persons throughout the world, in the above case, especially, from India. A reply was received from the White House stating that the President had asked NASA about the advisability of reopening UFO investigation but that NASA had replied that an investigation did not seem warranted "in light of the fact that there has been no concrete or new information about UFOs."

unidentified flying objects. Such revelations, based on information from the CIA, would be a reversal of official policy that in the past has downgraded UFO incidents.

As it became increasingly evident that no revelations were forthcoming from government agencies it was perhaps just a matter of time before some UFO study groups reacted under the provisions of the Freedom of Information Act.

In September 1977, William Spaulding, director of Ground Saucer Watch, Inc. (GSW), of Phoenix, Arizona, started the ball rolling by filing a Freedom of Information Act lawsuit against the CIA, alleging that the agency not only possessed thousands of documents about its involvement with UFO activity over the years but that it had actively conspired and was still conspiring to keep these documents secret from the public by actually denying their very existence.

GSW filed its suit as a result of refusal by the CIA to provide access to its UFO-related files on the grounds that national security was involved. GSW's strategy was to demand an ''in camera'' inspection (a private but official inspection carried out by a federal judge within the confines of his chambers) of documents to determine to what degree, if any, the nation's security was involved—a process provided for by the FOIA itself.

Then a second group, Citizens Against UFO Secrecy (CAUS), was formed early in 1978 under the directorship of W. T. Zechel, former research director of GSW and a onetime radio-telegraph operator for the Army Security Agency. CAUS's announced aim was nothing less than an ''attempt to establish that the USAF (or elements thereof) recovered a crashed extraterrestrial spacecraft'' in the Texas-

New Mexico-Mexico border area sometime in the late 1940s.

In December 1977, under the leadership of Brad Sparks, CAUS's technical consultant and director of research, the CAUS group completely assumed management of the pending GSW suit, and through discovery procedure and actual at-the-table negotiations succeeded in obtaining a court order from the U.S. District Court in Washington, D.C., which supposedly forced the CIA to do a file search for all its components for material relating to UFOs. Interestingly, some 10,000 pages of pertinent documents were reportedly "located" in July 1978, less than 900 pages of which were finally released to GSW/CAUS in December of that year. At the same time, the CIA refused to release some fifty-seven UFO-related *documents* (actual number of pages unknown) on the basis of national security regulations.

A similar request to the FBI by optical physicist Bruce Maccabee of Silver Spring, Maryland, eventually forced the FBI to produce nearly 1,000 pages of their UFO-related files, even after an initial denial that any such files existed.

Although most of the documents released thus far are copies of routine memoranda and the like which have produced little in the way of new or unexpected information, there are several which seem to have very strong implications with respect to the Roswell Incident. One of the most startling of these is a memo annotated by none other than the late J. Edgar Hoover, chief of the FBI, longtime powerful figure in government, and a person who was notably jealous both of his prerogatives and suspected infringements on his power. The memo was brief and to the point:

Memorandum for Mr. Ladd

Mr. [censored] also discussed this matter with Colonel L. R. Forney of MID [Military Intelligence Division]. Colonel Forney indicated that it was his attitude that inasmuch as it has been established that the flying discs are not the result of any Army or Navy experiments, the matter is of interest to the FBI. He stated that he was of the opinion that the Bureau, if at all possible, should accede to General Schulgen's request [i.e., to aid the Army Air Force in its investigations].

SWR:AJB [Initials]

Added to the bottom of the memo, in Hoover's own handwriting, is:

I would do it but before agreeing to it we must insist upon full access to discs recovered. For instance in the [illegible: could be either "SW" or "LA"] case the Army grabbed it and would not let us have it for cursory examination.

H.

One supposes that whatever further action was taken on this rather petulant demand is somewhere among the documents still (if ever) to be released. The fact that the memo is dated "July 15, 1947" is, however, highly significant, as is the uncertain reference to location which could be either "SW" (for Southwest) or "LA" (for Louisiana or perhaps even Los Angeles—the area in which Edwards Air Force Base is located).

The Louisiana possibility, which has been suggested by

some researchers in reference to a saucer hoax involving a sixteen-inch aluminum disc and some radio parts that took place in Shreveport on July 7, 1947, is almost totally ruled out by two FBI memos dealing with that case, one of which originates from the FBI Field Office in New Orleans and the other of which is from Hoover himself (both dated July 7). While Hoover's annotation above clearly indicates that he was referring to a crashed disc that "the Army grabbed . . . and would not let [the FBI] have" for examination, the two Louisiana memos referring to the Shreveport case plainly show that just the opposite was true and that the Army Air Force did indeed cooperate with the FBI on this case.

The evidence that Hoover was in fact referring to the New Mexico crash becomes even stronger in light of another FBI memo which was brought to the attention of the authors by researcher Brad Sparks. This one, a copy of an "Urgent" July 8, 1947, teletype communication between the FBI's Dallas Field Office and the Cincinnati Field Office, with copies to Hoover and the Strategic Air Command, refers directly to the Roswell Incident. Pertinent sections of this memo are as follows:

TELETYPE

FBI DALLAS   7-8-47   6-17 PM

DIRECTOR AND SAC, CINCINNATI URGENT FLYING DISC, IN-FORMATION CONCERNING. [Censored]. HEADQUARTERS EIGHTH AIR FORCE, TELEPHONICALLY ADVISED THIS OFFICE THAT AN OBJECT PURPORTING TO BE A FLYING DISC WAS RE COVERED [*sic*] NEAR ROSWELL, NEW MEXICO, THIS DATE. . . .[Censored] FURTHER ADVISED THAT THE OBJECT FOUND RESEMBLES A HIGH ALTITUDE WEATHER BALLOON WITH A RADAR REFLECTOR, *BUT THAT TELEPHONIC CONVERSATION BETWEEN THEIR OFFICE AND WRIGHT FIELD HAD NOT BORNE*

OUT THIS BELIEF. DISC AND BALLOON BEING TRANSPORTED TO WRIGHT FIELD BY SPECIAL PLANE FOR EXAMINATION. [Italics added] INFORMATION PROVIDED THIS OFFICE BECAUSE OF NATION٬١ INTEREST IN CASE AND FACT THAT NATIONAL BROADCASTING COMPANY٬ ASSOCIATED PRESS AND OTHERS ATTEMPTING TO BREAK STORY OF LOCATION OF DISC TODAY. [Censored] ADVISED WOULD REQUEST WRIGHT FIELD TO ADVISE CINCINNATI OFFICE RESULTS OF EXAMINATION. . . .

WYLY

END

Upon analysis of this all-important piece of communication, several points become immediately apparent:

(1) At no point was the FBI given access to the disc or wreckage recovered, exactly as indicated by Hoover's July 15 memo.

(2) Someone at Ramey's office at Fort Worth, probably Ramey himself, had conferred by telephone directly with Wright Field concerning the exact nature and description of the strange object that had fallen into their hands. The result of this conversation was the clear conclusion that whatever the object that had exploded over the Brazel ranch was, it was definitely *not* a "high altitude weather balloon with a radar reflector," in spite of the fact that certain elements of it may have in some ways resembled such a device.

(3) General Ramey's statement that the special flight to Wright Field had been canceled and that the debris was on the floor of his office and would probably remain right there was, as both Major Marcel and Colonel DuBose have already stated, a blatant and deliberate falsehood clearly designed by Ramey solely for the purpose of getting the press off of his back.

(4) The Army Air Force's apparent motive in informing the FBI about the case at all appears only to have been to ensure their assistance in quelling public reaction should NBC and AP have proven successful in their attempts to break the full extent of the story to the public.

If the AAF at Wright Field ever did advise the FBI of the results of their investigations concerning the disc, then such results have never been made public. The bureau's failure to obtain proper details about the Roswell Incident did not, however, dissuade Hoover from his conviction that the best way to gain as much information as possible about these mysterious discs was to cooperate with the AAF rather than to try and work around them. Accordingly, on July 30, 1947, the following directive was issued to all agents:

7-30-47
BUREAU BULLETIN No. 42
Series 1947

You should investigate each instance which is brought to your attention of a sighting of a flying disc in order to ascertain whether or not is. is [sic] a bona-fide sighting, an imaginary one or a prank. You should also bear in mind that individuals might report seeing flying discs for various reasons. It is conceivable that an individual might be desirous of seeking personal publicity, causing hysteria or playing a prank.

The Bureau should be notified immediately by teletype of all reported sightings and the results of your inquiries. In instances where the report appears to have merit, the teletype should be followed by a letter to the Bureau containing in detail the results of your inquiries. The Army Air Forces have assured the

Bureau complete cooperation in these matters and in any instances where they fail to make the information available to you or make the recovered discs available for your examination, it should promptly be brought to the attention of the Bureau.

Any information you develop in connection with these discs should be promptly brought to the attention of the Army through your usual liason [sic] channels.

62-83894

OFF. COPY FILED

252   70

58 AUG 18 1947   AUG 4, 1947

Even though the above documents clearly indicate extensive FBI involvement in the investigation of flying saucers, this involvement was later covered up and denied by the bureau. In the authors' possession are copies of several letters from the FBI dated between 1966 and 1972 and written in response to public inquiries regarding the nature and extent of the FBI's involvement with the flying-disc phenomenon. In each of these letters, all signed by J. Edgar Hoover, the stock response is given: "For your information, the investigation of Unidentified Flying Objects is not and never has been a matter that is within the investigative jurisdiction of the FBI."

Still another unexpected find turned up among the reports released. This was a memo, dated 23 September 1947, from General Nathan Twining of the Air Force and was sent by him as commander of the AAF Air Materiel Command, directed to the Air Technical Intelligence Command at Dayton, Ohio, which had apparently requested his office for guidance about "flying discs." An excerpt from this memo follows:

23 September 1947

Subject: *AMC Opinion Concerning "Flying Discs"*

TO: *Commanding General*
Army Air Forces
Washington 25, D.C.

ATTENTION: Brig. General George
Schulgen
AC/AS-2

1. As requested by AC/AS-2 there is presented below the considered opinion of this Command concerning the so-called "Flying Discs." This opinion is based on interrogation report data furnished by AC/AS-2 and preliminary studies by personnel of T-2 and Aircraft Laboratory, Engineering Division T-3. This opinion was arrived at in a conference between personnel from the Air Institute of Technology, Intelligence T-2, Office Chief of Engineering Division, and the Aircraft, Power Plant and Propeller Laboratories of Engineering Division T-3.

2. It is the opinion that:

a. *The phenomenon reported is something real and not visionary or fictitious.*

b. *There are objects probably approximately the shape of a disc, of such appreciable size as to appear to be as large as man-made aircraft.*

c. There is a possibility that some of the incidents may be caused by natural phenomenon, such as meteors.

d. The reported operating characteristics such as extreme rates of climb, maneuverability (particularly in roll), and action which must be considered evasive when sighted or contacted by friendly aircraft and radar, lend belief to the possibility that *some of the objects are controlled either manually, automatically or remotely.*

e. The apparent *common description* of the objects is as follows:

(1) *Metallic or light reflecting surface.*

(2) Absence of trail, except in a few instances when the object apparently was operating under high performance conditions.

(3) *Circular or elliptical in shape, flat on bottom and domed on top.*

(4) Several reports of well kept formation flights varying from three to nine objects.

(5) Normally no associated sound, except in three instances a substantial rumbling roar was noted. . . .

It is understandable that the Twining memo makes no reference to the Roswell disc, but the date of the document, barely two and a half months after the incident, and the fact that the memo accepts the reality of "flying discs" are indicative of the official climate of urgency generated by the Roswell Incident.

On the question raised in the CAUS action re specific date relating to the matter of a UFO crash and recovery operation (or operations), however, the CIA responded in August that "such data would fall under Air Force purview and such data would have to be obtained from the USAF."

Anticipating just such a response, CAUS had already filed a FOIA request with the Air Force the month before specifically requesting crashed-saucer records for 1947–48 and listing as participants in the incident a retired USAF colonel who reportedly "was in charge of securing the area during the recovery operation" and a retired lieutenant colonel who had been airborne at the time of the alleged crash and had been alerted to the object's intrusion into U.S. air space by radio reports over his aircraft's scramble frequency.

The Air Force confirmed that the first individual, identified only as "Colonel John Bowen," had indeed been serving as provost marshal at *Carswell Air Force Base, Fort Worth* at the time of the alleged incident, but would provide no additional information. In August, a *pro forma* denial was issued in which the Air Force characteristically denied the existence of documents or records relating to the crash and recovery of any extraterrestrial device.

Later, responding to a subsequent appeal of this denial filed under the provisions of the FOIA, the Air Force maintained that it was not subject to receive such an appeal since it had not denied access to documents but rather had denied the very existence of such material. The FOIA, it said, contemplated only cases involving the denial of access to records, *not* cases where the specific existence of records is denied.

And there the matter temporarily rests. As of the time of this writing, a prestigious Washington, D.C., law firm, anticipating a long struggle, has agreed to handle the CAUS vs. Air Force crashed-UFO suit at a reduced fee rate as a "public interest action," while at the same time the GSW/CIA case is proceeding through the courts in the hands of a New York law firm. Peter Gersten, the attorney in charge of the case, is not overly sanguine about the material the action has so far produced: "We suspect that the agency is withholding at least two hundred more documents than the fifty-seven they have admitted they are keeping from us to protect intelligence sources." He plans, nevertheless, to pursue the suit from agency to agency until the missing reports (including those of the Roswell Incident) are obtained.

But on the surface, at least, the climate of official

cooperation has undergone a recent temperate change. Requests for information about UFOs are now being met or at least acknowledged with considerable alacrity. Exceptions must be made, of course, for the important cases of which the happening at Roswell may be classified as a key and, in a way, as a preview of the future.

Consider the implications of the Roswell Incident: If only *one* of the many individuals mentioned in this book who claim to have witnessed the crash and/or subsequent recovery of an extraterrestrial vehicle is telling the truth—then perhaps at this very moment we sit at the verge of the greatest news story of the twentieth century, the first contact with live (or dead) extraterrestrials. This occurrence, if true, would be at least comparable to Columbus's encounter with the startled natives on his visit to the New World. Except for one thing. In this case *we* would be the startled natives.

9

The Russian Connection

From the dusty newspaper files of other decades we learn of a tremendous and unexplained explosion of a meteor or comet which crashed into the earth from the skies over Siberia in 1908; from the high Andean plateau of South America reports come to us of a recent fireball that sheared off the top of a mountain in 1979; in 1978 tremendous unidentified booms were heard from over the Atlantic Ocean off the coasts of New Jersey and Virginia; shattering booms or explosions were also referred to in news reports of the nineteenth century. The NASA, AEC, FAC, NOAA, Air Force, Coast Guard, Navy, and other concerned agencies have all given explanations of what the booms were *not* but failed to establish in each case what they were. Nor have explanations for the following phenomena been satisfactorily established: The Siberian, or Tunguska, fireball, exploding spaceship, atomic blast, or whatever it was left no trace of extraterrestrial or meteor core. There remained only a flattened or burned part of the forest (but *no* crater), a considerable number of dead reindeer, local legends of a great explosion, and residual radiation which lasted through the years.

Proof of the Andean incident, reputedly in Bolivia, is still as tenuous as the mountain air, while the mighty booms of 1978 off the Atlantic Coast may have come from space or from the earth itself. And, besides the above suppositions of possible crashes and explosions from space there exist other rumors usually dealing with downed UFOs in the United States which may, of course, be variants of the original Roswell Incident improved and relocated with retelling. Apparently nothing further has surfaced in the intervening years which has left a more concrete trace of extraterrestrial visitors than certain burned sections of woodland and the unexplained searing of the desert floor.

In the past several years, however, rumors and a certain amount of semiofficial documentation have been surfacing in regard to another "visitor from space." This one left some concrete proof of its encounter with earth, during which the UFO apparently suffered an explosion and subsequently struck the earth before it recovered and was able to resume its path in the sky. There exist certain similarities between this Russian occurrence, which allegedly took place near Lake Onega in the Karelean Associated Soviet Socialist Republic, U.S.S.R., and the Roswell Incident.

The Lake Onega incident took place in 1961 but only recently have references to it appeared in the West. It is described in *UFOs in the U.S.S.R., Vol. II* (1975) by Professor Felix Ziegel and in *The New Soviet Psychic Discoveries* by Gris and Dick (Prentice Hall, 1978). Original reports* at the time of the incident were made by

---

*Part of the material relating to the Lake Onega incident, described in this chapter, was translated directly from the Russian notes of Professor Ziegel by William Moore.

Professor Ziegel, of the Soviet Aviation Institute, and Yuri Fomin, a Soviet state engineer. It is noteworthy that before official reports began to be circulated in the Soviet Union considerable comment on this occurrence had appeared in illegal *samisdat,* or underground, publications, just as if reports of nonofficial UFO publications in the United States had later been officially credited by the government. The latter has not yet happened.

The incident occurred near the now-abandoned village of Entino on the far northern shores of Lake Onega. In the early morning of April 27, 1961, a group of twenty-five hunters and woodsmen saw an "aerial object of unknown origin" approach the ground and then collide with it on an inlet bay. (According to witnesses, this happened at 8 or 10 A.M. Reported time variation might have been due to several reasons, such as confusion between Moscow and local time, often a problem in the Soviet Union, the probability that the hunters were not wearing watches, and the understandable nervousness of Soviet citizens faced with explosions coming from the sky. But the descriptions of the witnesses agreed exactly as to what they had seen.)

The object was oval-shaped, as big as a large passenger plane, and glowed with a blue-green light. It was traveling at a low altitude and at tremendous speed. It was on an east-to-west course when it struck the ground near the northern shoreline of the lake, making a sound like a large explosion and causing considerable damage to the ground and surrounding vegetation.

The alarmed party of hunters contacted the forest ranger for the district, Valentin Borsky, with an urgent request for assistance. Borsky arrived on the scene at about eight the following morning.

Further investigation by Borsky revealed that other people in the area had observed the same sequence of events as the hunters. According to witnesses, the object had survived the impact with the earth and continued westward with a slightly wobbling motion on a trajectory still very close to the ground. Then it had disappeared. All witnesses reported no sound associated with the object except for the noise of the impact itself.

Subsequent investigation of the impact site by Borsky and later by a combined civilian-military team from the town of Povenets, with environmental scientist Fydor Denisov heading the civilian contingent and Soviet Army engineer Major Anton Kopeikin in command of the military section with senior technician Lieutenant Boris Lapunov, revealed that the object's collision with the lakeshore had produced three trenches, one major and two lesser ones, with accompanying uprooting of vegetation. The impact on the ice itself had smashed a large area of lake ice, overturning several huge chunks of it and throwing a number of other large and small pieces out into the ground. The ice appeared to have acquired an intense green coloring from the impact. The trenches produced on the escarpment along the shore consisted of a major trench some twenty-seven meters long, fifteen meters wide, and with a maximum depth of three meters; a second trench, starting at the far western end of the first and separated from it by about five and a half meters, and a third less-defined trench some forty centimeters in width and leading to the lake itself. The escarpment at this point of the lake is inclined about sixty degrees to the surface of the lake. Beyond the three trench-like marks mentioned and the impact damage sustained by the lake ice, there appeared to be no other evidence of collision in the area.

A close examination of the trenches along the escarpment and the uprooted ground on the shore of the lake was conducted by Major Kopeikin. This led to the recovery of a number of tiny, black, metallic-looking, geometrically shaped particles of apparently artificial origin, and one small piece of a thin, metallic-looking *foil-like* (author's emphasis) substance, one millimeter thick, two centimeters long, and a half centimeter wide, later found to be of the same composition as the black particles. These, along with a number of samples of the bright ''chrome-green'' colored ice and the black grains, were collected and subsequently sent to the Leningrad Technological Institute for analysis.

The analysis produced the following results:

A. The green ice, when melted, left behind a residue of stringlike fiber. This fiber, when analyzed, yielded an unknown organic compound accompanied by the presence of small quantities of aluminum, calcium, barium, silicon, sodium, and titanium.
B. The geometrically shaped metallic-appearing particles were found to be resistant to acid and high temperatures, were not radioactive, and seemed to consist of a silicon-iron alloy in combination with lesser amounts of aluminum, lithium, titanium, and sodium.
C. The foil-like substance appeared to be of the same composition as the larger particles.

The noted Soviet geophysicist Professor Vladimir Sharanov of the Leningrad Technological Institute became so interested in the incident that he made arrangements to visit the isolated site himself. Basing his conclusions on the above analysis as well as on the evidence at the collision site, Professor Sharanov expressed his opinion as follows:

> I do not believe that the object was a meteorite.
> The destruction and disturbance to the ground caused

by falling meteorites was absent in this case. Specifically, a falling meteorite leaves a crater two to five
times its size. In this case no craters could be found.
The descent of a meteorite is accompanied by clearly
identifiable audible and visual effects. There were
none in this case.

Finally, the chemical substance left by meteorites
in the ground was not present in this case.

The grains found on the lake bottom, while unex-
plainable at the present time, were clearly of artificial
origin.

The possibility that the object may have been a regular
aircraft or even an American spy plane (a normal reaction
in the U.S.S.R.), reconnoitering at a very low altitude in
order to escape radar detection, was totally ruled out by
Sharanov and by scientists at the Leningrad Institute. They
concluded that no known aircraft could possibly have with-
stood such a heavy impact against frozen ground without
suffering severe structural damage and losing significant
numbers of its parts, which would have subsequently been
located in the area.

Professor Felix Ziegel is a respected Soviet space scientist and astronomer and, having written some twenty-eight
books on astronomy and astronautics and numerous scientific papers on these subjects, would seem to be eminently
capable of and understandably careful in establishing the
difference between aircraft, comets, and meteors. His own
conclusions about the unidentified flying object of Lake
Onega, based on his personal investigation of the case, is
of considerable interest. He qualifies it as "a space probe,
coming from another planet [which had] scraped the ground
but managed to continue despite presumably superficial
damage." He continues: "It is the only such case on

record within the territory of the U.S.S.R.'' Professor Ziegel, in his above observations, was obviously referring only to ''crash'' contacts and not the many sightings of UFOs over the U.S.S.R., including brief encounters with fighter planes, sometimes with fatal results for the Soviet pilots.

Professor Aleksander Kazentsev, a noted Russian scientific investigator and writer and a member of the Soviet Academy of Science, was somewhat more direct: ''It was obviously a space probe. If you tried to identify it as anything else you would find that all evidence points to the contrary. Obviously the files on the Onega mystery are far from closed.''

The Roswell and Lake Onega incidents seem to be coincidentally similar. Consider the ingredients: An unknown object flying east to west at an extremely low altitude and at very high speed; there occurs a collision or explosion, producing damage to the ground, uprooting vegetation, and, in the Lake Onega case, ice; metallic-like debris is scattered over the area; no sound is heard except that of the collision, impact, or explosion; the object remains in the air, still traveling west after its close encounter with the ground, although in the Roswell Incident it crash-landed after the first malfunction.

But did the Lake Onega object sustain enough damage to cause it to crash to the earth at some point farther to the west as the Roswell object seems to have done? Given the extremely vast area and small concentration of population in the area surrounding the Lake Onega impact site, such an event could easily have occurred and the resultant wreckage could still be awaiting discovery by some fur trapper, woodcutter, wandering tribesman, or possibly a member of a work gang. It is also possible, since the population is so sparse, that the wreckage of such an object (and possibly bodies of the crew) could have been detected and recovered by Soviet military units without the civilization population becoming aware of it, a situation certainly more likely in the U.S.S.R. than in the U.S.A., where the Roswell Incident got announced in the press and on the radio before the news was circumvented by the authorities.

For decades the U.S.A. and the U.S.S.R. have suspected each other of being the source of the unfathomable and persistent UFOs. A large segment of public opinion in both superpowers is now more or less convinced that our mysterious visitors really exist and that they come from somewhere else in space, or perhaps in time. Now, as both powers are beginning to explore our nearest neighbor in the cosmos, the moon, it would seem advisable that the two powers, and others who eventually join the exploration of the moon, share information attained, especially regarding the possibility of present or past life on the moon.

There are persistent rumors that U.S. astronauts and Soviet cosmonauts have observed and photographed what appear to be constructions on the surface of the moon. These include walls, domes, bridge-like formations, spires and spire-like pyramids estimated to be 150 feet high within the Sea of Storms, where Conrad and Gordon also observed "something resembling a rectilinear wall." On the dark side of the moon the Soviet Luna 9 reported geometric arrangements of huge stones, which, according to Professor Ivanov, a Soviet space scientist, *could* be flight markers for a lunar runway. Within the Sea of Tranquility a number of sharp shadows seem to be caused by precipitous towering structures, one shadow described as indicating a tower-like formation "as high as the Washington Monument." Still another resembling a gigantic antenna at the edge of the Jansen Crater is described as being of "improbable height" with the added suggestion that it might be a gigantic electric pylon.

Such rumors or reports have been, of course, regularly denied or, when already photographed, downgraded as perfectly natural formations. Astronomers and photo interpreters, understandably careful of their reputations, have explained the pyramids as shadows, the bridges and walls as curving ridges, the arrangements of stones as chance scattering of boulders, and the domes as the bubbling up of the moon's surface because of volcanic activity. (But if this were truly the case the surface of the domes themselves would be the same color as the surrounding moonscape and not, as they are, a translucent white.)

Further unexplained phenomena noted on the moon imply motion. One photograph (reportedly from the Apollo 11 mission), published in the United States, the United Kingdom, and other countries, shows two glowing unidentified discs moving up from a moon crater. Sustained bursts of lights and intermittent moon spots glowing in changing colors have long been observed on different parts of the moon by a large selection of astronomers observing from different parts of the earth and at different times. These have been especially noted as coming from the Cobra's Head in Schroter Valley and in the Aristarchus and Maskelyne craters. The observed phenomenon of a curious silicon-like mist occasionally seen rising from the surface of the moon has been ascribed by one observer, considering the absence of water vapor, to the possibility that "moon-movers" were digging in one of the craters. These last mentioned phenomena, if further verified, would doubtlessly be ascribed to the still slightly active interior of the moon.

If we adopt, however, the logical supposition that we

are not alone in our galaxy it is not too much an additional step of the imagination to speculate on the possibility of the use of the moon by unspecified others as a base from which to observe our earth. The dark side of the moon presents several outstanding advantages to this end. It is shielded from radio interference from earth, it has no climactic difficulties or corrosion problems, and, as the largest moon in the solar system relative to the size of its planet—almost a sister planet to the earth—it is conveniently near the developed planetary life existing on earth.

Physicist Stanton Friedman has suggested that perhaps the relatively small UFOs are "exploration modules" brought to the moon by larger craft from other points in this or other galaxies.

The tens of thousands of UFOs that have been reported throughout the earth began in 1947 shortly after the atom bomb ushered in the era which might be labeled "the end of cosmic isolation" or "the end of innocence." The proximity of intensive UFO sightings and past atomic bombings and continuing tests may have provoked a more lively interest in atomic activity on earth on the part of our neighbors (if we take it for granted that they exist) in outer or inner space and intensified their observations and patrols, especially over the extensive land areas where the great powers are busily preparing for atomic warfare.

It is logical to consider that since the great number of sightings seem to have been noted over the U.S.A. and its adjoining oceans and, more recently, an increasing number over the plains and forests of the U.S.S.R., there should have been occasional malfunctions in the operations of UFOs over these two extensive world areas. While there seem to have been at least two instances that have left materials behind, there might have been still others that both sides are keeping secret from each other and from their own people.

The danger of continued UFO secrecy, now being tested in the courts of the United States, is fairly obvious. Individual UFO malfunction resulting in large explosions or retaliatory attacks by UFOs could easily be attributed to potential enemy action (since UFOs do not officially exist) and set off chain reactions leading to the use of nuclear warheads among the increasing number of nations possessing these weapons. The nations of the earth owe it to themselves and each other to share information received on UFOs over the skies of earth as well as evidence of unidentified nonearthly activities in space.

Werner von Braun, the noted father of rocketry who helped develop the V-2 for Germany in WW II and later the U.S. space shots, made a prophetic statement before his death about the pervasive but hard-to-establish quality of UFOs and their inference about extraterrestrial life: ''It is as impossible to confirm them in the present as it will be to deny them in the future.''

Let us hope that as our present becomes our uncertain future we will be ready to accept them in understanding and goodwill and, at the same time, with the necessary technical preparation, on earth as well as in space.

For this we need a common global space effort, a free exchange between scientific and technological establishments throughout the world. It will be necessary to share our knowledge and inventive techniques, to inform the public of what is happening, and to contribute as much as possible to a safe progression of our shared spaceship, Earth, through the dangers inherent in the cosmos. And while we do not yet know whether UFOs represent a danger, it is nevertheless self-evident, as the great powers of earth experiment with ever-longer-ranging missiles and killer satellites, that humanity represents a danger to itself in space as well as on the earth.

The increasingly obvious presence of UFOs over the continents and oceans of earth give us cause to reflect on the use we may make of our great advances in science developed in the last century and possibly now getting out of hand.

Many motives have been ascribed to the senders or occupants of UFOs, mostly concerned with attack, exploitation, reconnaissance for conquest, capture of human specimens, or planned future occupation of the earth, all of which mirror our own images of how *we* would react in their place. But, possibly because of the danger we represent to ourselves and our surroundings, there may be another explanation. Perhaps what we call UFOs are part of a design—or message—whose meaning may become clear to us, one hopes, while there is still time.

Acknowledgments

The authors wish to express their sincere thanks and appreciation to each of the following individuals and organizations whose contributions of time, information, assistance, and cooperation have made this book possible. In alphabetical order:

Walter H. Andrus, Jr.—UFO researcher; Director, Mutual UFO Network

Gray Barker—author, editor, publisher

Lt. Col. Robert J. Barrowclough, USAF-ret.

Norman Bean—electronics engineer, researcher, UFO lecturer

Lin Berlitz—researcher

Valerie Berlitz—author, artist

William Blanchard—attorney-at-law

David Branch—writer, researcher, journalist

Shirley Brazel

William Brazel—geoseismologist, rancher
Larry Bryant—researcher; Director of CAUS
Holm Bursum, Jr.—banker
Maurice Chatelain—author, computer scientist
Reilly H. Crabb—Director of BSRF, lecturer, publisher, researcher
Calvin Denton—banker
Brig. Gen. Thomas J. DuBose, USAF-ret.
Larry Fenwick—UFO researcher, Director of Canadian UFO Research Network (CUFORN)
John Fox—banker
Stanton T. Friedman—nuclear physicist, UFO researcher, writer, lecturer
John A. Gardner—real estate agent
Laura Gardner—administrative assistant, Notary Public
Peter Gersten—attorney-at-law
Capt. Walter Golden, USAF-ret.
The Honorable Barry Goldwater, U.S. Senator (Arizona); general, USAF-ret.
Flight Major Hughie Green, RCAF-ret.—author, actor
Walter Haut—proprietor, WH Art Gallery
Dr. Frank Hibben, Ph.D.—archaeologist
Ramona Kashe—Chief of Research for Charles Berlitz, Washington, D.C.
E. J. LaFave, Jr.—banker
General Curtis LeMay, USAF-ret.
Jim and Coral Lorenzen—Aerial Phenomena Research Organization (APRO)
Dr. Bruce Maccabee, Ph.D.—optical physicist
Gary C. Magnuson—educator
Nic Magnuson—researcher
Ruth Magnuson—nurse's aide
Jean Swedmark Maltais
L. W. "Vern" Maltais—Veterans Service Officer

Dr. Jesse Marcel, M.D.—physician
Lt. Col. Jesse A. Marcel, USAF-ret.
C. B. Moore—aerologist, atmospheric physicist
Rita Mulcahy—librarian
Ted Phillips—UFO researcher
Dennis Pilichis—publisher, editor, Director of UFO Information Network (UFOIN)
Mr. and Mrs. Floyd Proctor—ranchers
Clint Saltmeir—rancher
Jean Schaub
Lawrence Schaub—highway engineer
Alice P. Scully—writer
Brad Sparks—author, researcher
Hal Starr—researcher, lecturer, radio reporter
Otto Alexander Steen—engineer, archivist, lecturer
Leonard H. Stringfield—public relations director, UFO researcher, author
Brig. Gen. Woodrow P. Swancutt, USAF-ret.
Jack Swickard—journalist, editor
J. Manson Valentine—explorer, archaeologist, writer, UFO researcher
Dr. Bernard H. Wailes, Ph.D.—archaeologist
Dr. Robert C. Wykoff, Ph.D.—consulting physicist

And a special thank you to the following:
Janie and Robert Anderson
Pearl and Henry Applbaum
Clarence Barrett
Anne Blanchard
Paul Brazel
Alice Crider
Mr. and Mrs. J. F. Danley
Carl Erickson
Lorraine (Brazel) Ferguson

Dale Flournoy
Lee Garner
Mick Georgin
Christopher Green
John L. Greenwald
Edward Gregory
Loren Gross
Rolla Hinkel
Alice Knight
Mike McClellan
Paul McEvoy
Art McQuiddy
Lynne A. "Lee" Moore
D. M. and W. L. Moore, Sr.
Irving Newton
Robert R. Porter
Bessie (Brazel) Schreiber
Emily Simms
Lydia Sleppy
Dr. O. M. Solandt, Ph. D.
Jim Sweet
Merle Tucker
George Walsh
Jimmy Ward
Walt Whitmore, Jr.
Charles Wilhelm
and the several others who desire to remain anonymous.

Organizations:

Aerial Phenomena Research Organization, Inc. (APRO), Tucson, Ariz.
American Meteorological Society, Boston, Mass.

Associated Press (AP), New York

Borderland Sciences Research Foundation (BSRF), Vista, Calif.

Citizens Against UFO Secrecy (CAUS), Arlington, Va.

Denver Public Library

Federal Bureau of Investigation, Washington, D.C. (and Field Offices: Cincinnati, Dallas, El Paso, and Albuquerque)

Group I pictures, Hollywood, Calif.

Los Angeles Public Library

Lujan-Stedman Funeral Home, Socorro, N. Mex.

Minneapolis Public Library

Morris (Minn.) Public Library

Mutual UFO Network (MUFON), Seguin, Tex.

National Archives, Washington, D.C.

National Radio Astronomy, VLA Program, Socorro, N. Mex.

New Mexico Institute of Mining & Technology, Socorro, N. Mex.

New York (City) Public Library

Phoenix Public Library

Prescott (Ariz.) Public Library

Roswell (N. Mex.) Public Library

San Francisco Public Library

Socorro City Police Department (N. Mex.)

Socorro County Sheriff's Office

Socorro Public Library

Tucumcari (N. Mex.) Public Library

UFO Information Network (UFOIN), Rome, Ohio

United States Air Force

United States Geological Survey, Denver, Colo.

University of Minnesota (Wilson) Library, Minneapolis

University of Minnesota (Morris Campus) Library

University of Pennsylvania Museum, Philadelphia

Newspapers:
(Most generally for applicable dates in July 1947)

Albuquerque (N. Mex.) *Journal*
Amarillo (Tex.) *Globe*
Arizona *Daily Star* (Tucson)
Baltimore *Sun*
Bisbee (Ariz.) *Daily Review*
Chicago *Daily News*
Chicago *Sun*
Dallas *Daily Times Herald*
Dallas *Morning Sun*
Detroit *News*
Fort Worth *Star-Telegram*
Lincoln County (N. Mex.) *News*
London (England) *Times*
Los Angeles *Daily Mirror*
Los Angeles *Daily News*
Los Angeles *Times*
Louisville (Ky.) *Courier Journal*
National Enquirer
New York *Daily News*
New York *Herald Tribune*
New York *Times*
New York *World-Telegram*
Pittsburgh *Press*
Pittsburgh *Sun Telegraph*
Portland (Oreg.) *Oregonian*
Roswell (N. Mex.) *Daily Record*
St. Louis *Post-Dispatch*
San Francisco *Chronicle*
San Francisco *Examiner*
Socorro (N. Mex.) *Defensor-Chieftain*
Tucumcari (N. Mex.) *Daily News*
Washington (D. C.) *Post*

Bibliography

Books, Magazines, and Other Publications:

Barker, Gray. "America's Captured Flying Saucers—Cover-up of the Century," *UFO Report* (May 1977), p. 32 ff.

Cahn, J. P. "The Flying Saucer and the Mysterious Little Men," *True* (September 1952), p. 17.

———"The Flying Saucer Swindlers," *True* (December 1955), p. 66.

Carr, Prof. R. S. (letter from), in "Contact," *Official UFO* (February 1976), p. 8.

Chatelain, Maurice. *Our Ancestors Came From Outer Space.* New York: Doubleday, 1977.

Crabb, Reilly H. *Flying Saucers at Edwards AFB.* Vista, Calif.: BSRF Press, n.d.

Davidson, Dr. Leon, Ph.D., ed. *Flying Saucers, An Analysis of Air Force Project Blue Book Special Report No. 14.* Clarksburg, W. Va.: Saucerian Press, 1971.

Faucher, Eric; Goodstein, Ellen; and Gris, Henry. "Alien UFOs Watched Our First Astronauts on the Moon." *National Enquirer* (September 12, 1979), p. 25.

"Flying Saucer Hoax," *Saturday Review of Literature* (December 6, 1952), p. 6.

Gelatt, Roland. "Saucer from Venus," *Saturday Review of Literature* (September 23, 1950), p. 20.

Hall, Richard H., ed. *The UFO Evidence.* Washington, D.C.: NICAP, 1964.

"History of the 8th Air Force, Ft. Worth, Texas" (microfilm). National Archives, Washington, D.C.

"History of Roswell Army Air Force, 427th Base Unit & 509th Bomb Group (VH), combined," (microfilm). National Archives, Washington, D.C.

Hurt, W. R. Jr.; and McKnight, Daniel. "Archaeology of the San Agustin Plains," *American Antiquity,* XIV, 3 (July 1949), pp. 172–94.

Huyghe, Patrick. "UFO Files: The Untold Story," New York *Times Magazine* (October 14, 1979), p. 106.

Jacobs, Dr. David M., Ph.D. *The UFO Controversy in America.* Bloomington, Indiana: Indiana University Press, 1975.

Just Cause (Newsletter of the Citizens Against UFO Secrecy), Numbers 1–9.

LePoer-Trench, Brinsley. *Flying Saucers Have Arrived.* New York: World Publishing Co., 1970.

McClellan, Mike. "The UFO Crash of '48 is a Hoax," *Official UFO* (October 1975), p. 36.

"People of the Week—Dwight Eisenhower," *U.S. News & World Report* (February 26, 1954), p. 6.

"Pies in the Sky," *Time* (April 3, 1950), p. 36.

"Presidency, The," *Time* (March 1, 1954), pp. 12–13.

R.A.A.F. Yearbook, Roswell (N.M.) Army Air Base, 1947.

Scully, Frank. *Behind the Flying Saucers*. New York: Holt, 1950.

Stringfield, Leonard H. "Retrievals of the Third Kind [revised version]." *MUFON UFO Journal* (July and August 1978).

————*Situation Red: UFO Siege*. New York: Doubleday, 1978.

"United States of Dreamland, The," *Doubt* (The Fortean Society Magazine), No. 19 (November 1947), pp. 282–90.

"Visitors from Venus," *Time* (January 9, 1950), p. 49.

Index